T0352115

PORTRAIT
OF A LIFE

PORTRAIT OF A LIFE

Melanie Klein and the Artists

Roger Amos

PHOENIX
PUBLISHING HOUSE
firing the mind

First published in 2019 by
Phoenix Publishing House Ltd
62 Bucknell Road
Bicester
Oxfordshire OX26 2DS

British Library Cataloguing in Publication Data

A C.I.P. for this book is available from the British Library

ISBN-13: 978-1-912691-41-8

Edited, designed, and produced by Communication Crafts, East Grinstead

Printed in the United Kingdom

www.firingthemind.com

For Anne and our children
Howard, Rachel, and Josephine

CONTENTS

LIST OF FIGURES   ix

PREFACE   xiii

ABOUT THE AUTHOR   xvii

Chapter One
Melanie Klein, portraits, and art   1

Chapter Two
Early life, childhood, and adolescence
Vienna, 1882 to 1902   13

Chapter Three
Married life
Budapest, 1903 to 1913   29

Chapter Four
The unrecorded decade
Budapest and Berlin, 1914 to 1925   45

Chapter Five
Middle years
London, 1926 to 1950 51

Chapter Six
Later life
London, 1951 to 1960 81

REFERENCES 123
INDEX 129

LIST OF FIGURES

1   The Reizes children. Melanie, aged 6 (*c*.1888). *Unknown*   15
    photographer, the Wimmer Studio, Vienna

2   Melanie Klein, aged 8 (*c*.1890). *Unknown photographer, the Olga*   17
    Studio, Vienna

3   Melanie Klein, aged 8 (*c*.1890). *Unknown photographer, the Olga*   18
    Studio, Vienna

4   Melanie Klein, aged 16 (*c*.1898). *Unknown photographer, the Carl*   19
    Pietzner Studio, Vienna

5   Melanie Klein, aged 18 (1900). *Unknown photographer; the Carl*   20
    Pietzner Studio, Vienna

6   Melanie Klein, aged 18 (*c*.1900). *Unknown photographer, the Carl*   21
    Pietzner Studio, Vienna

7   Melanie Klein, aged 20 (*c*.1902). *Unknown photographer, the Carl*   22
    Pietzner Studio, Vienna

8   Melanie Klein, aged 20 (*c*.1902). *Unknown photographer, the Carl*   23
    Pietzner Studio, Vienna

9   Melanie Klein, aged 20 (*c*.1902). *Unknown photographer, the Carl*   24
    Pietzner Studio, Vienna

10 Arthur Klein, aged 18 (1896). *Unknown photographer, Zurich*   25

11   Dr Arthur Klein, aged 24 (1902). *Unknown photographer, Boston,*   26
      Massachusetts

12   Emanuel Reizes, aged 17 (1894). *Unknown photographer, the Olga*   27
      Studio, Vienna

13   Emanuel Reizes, aged 24 (1901). *Unknown photographer*   28

14   Melanie Klein, aged 23 (1905). *Unknown photographer, the Hegedüs*   30
      Studio, Budapest

15   Melanie Klein, aged 26 (*c*.1908);. *Unknown photographer, the*   31
      Hegedüs Studio, Budapest

16   The Klein family (*c*.1908). *Unknown photographer*   33

17   Melanie Klein, aged 28 (*c*.1910). *Unknown photographer, Budapest*   34

18   Melanie Klein, aged 28 (*c*.1910). *Unknown photographer, Budapest*   35

19   Melanie Klein, aged 28 (*c*.1910). *Unknown photographer, Budapest*   36

20   Melanie Klein, aged 28 (*c*.1910). *Unknown photographer, Budapest*   37

21   Melanie Klein, aged 29 (*c*.1911). *Possibly taken by János Szabó,*   38
      Budapest

22   Melanie Klein, aged 29 (*c*.1911). *Possibly taken by János Szabó,*   39
      Budapest

23   Melanie Klein, aged 30 (*c*.1912–13). *Aladár Székely , Budapest*   40

24   Aladár Székely (date unknown). *Unknown photographer*   42

25   Melanie Klein, aged 42 (1924). *Róbert Berény, drawn at the 8th*   48
      International Psychoanalytical Congress, Salzburg, 1924

26   Herbert Lambert in his mid-40s (late 1920s). *Self-portrait*   52

27   Herbert Lambert, aged 47 (1929). *F & B Goodwin*   53

28   Melanie Klein, aged 45 (1927). *Herbert Lambert, Elliot and Fry's*   55
      Studio, London

29   Oscar Nemon and Sigmund Freud (1931). *Unknown photographer,*   57
      Vienna

30   Oscar Nemon and his statue of Freud (1969). *Falcon Stuart (Oscar*   58
      Nemon's son)

31   Oscar Nemon, aged 33 (1939). *Unknown photographer; possibly*   65
      Jessie Stonor

32   Oscar Nemon and Melanie Klein, London (1939). *Unknown*   67
      photographer; possibly Jessie Stonor

33 Low-relief sculptures of Melanie Klein, aged 57 (1939). *Sculptor* 68
    Oscar Nemon; restored by Jim Kempton, 2018; photograph taken by
    Sarah Lane

34 Oscar Nemon and Domenico Borghese (1924). *Unknown* 69
    photographer

35 Melanie Klein, aged 62 (1944). *Bertl Sachsel, London* 70

36 Melanie Klein, aged 62 (1944). *Bertl Sachsel, London* 71

37 Olga Dormandi (*c.*1948). *Self-portrait* 74

38 Oscar Nemon and Sándor Ferenczi (1931). *Unknown photographer* 76

39 Melanie Klein, aged 66 (*c.*1948). *Olga Dormandi, London* 77

40 Douglas Glass (late 1950s). *Self-portrait* 83

41 Melanie Klein, aged 70 (1952). *Douglas Glass, London* 84

42 Melanie Klein, aged 70 (1952). *Douglas Glass, London* 85

43 Melanie Klein, aged 70 (1952). *Douglas Glass, London* 86

44 William Coldstream (1956). *Walter Stoneman, London* 87

45 *Man with a Beard* (1939). *William Coldstream* 91

46 *Havildar Ajmer Singh* (1943). *William Coldstream* 92

47 Melanie Klein, aged 70 (1952). *William Coldstream* (*photograph of* 97
    the unfinished painting, taken by Ann Stokes)

48 Feliks Topolski (1954). *Edward Russell Westwood, London* 105

49 Melanie Klein, aged 75 (*c.*1957). *Feliks Topolski, London* 106

50 Melanie Klein, aged 75 (*c.*1957). *Feliks Topolski, London* 107

51 Melanie Klein, aged 75 (*c.*1957). *Feliks Topolski, London* 108

52 Melanie Klein, aged 75 (1957). *Hans Thorner, London* 112

53 Melanie Klein, aged 75 (1957). *Hans Thorner, London* 113

54 Melanie Klein, aged 75 (1957). *Hans Thorner, London* 114

55 Melanie Klein, aged 75 (1957). *Hans Thorner, London* 115

56 Jane Bown (1986). *Yevonde Middleton, London* 117

57 Melanie Klein, aged 77 (1959). *Jane Bown, London* 119

58 Melanie Klein, aged 77 (1959). *Jane Bown, London* 120

59 Melanie Klein, aged 77 (1959). *Jane Bown, London* 121

This exploration of the portraits of Melanie Klein stemmed from a chance observation: the Melanie Klein Trust is in possession of a brief, silent cine film showing Melanie Klein walking in her sunlit garden at Clifton Hill with a man who, at the time, was unidentified. It was my wife who realised that this man was, in fact, the sculptor Oscar Nemon, identified from a photograph in Phyllis Grosskurth's biography of Klein. Why was Oscar Nemon in conversation with Melanie Klein in her garden in 1939? What did the artist and the psychoanalyst make of each other? Why did Klein "loathe" the sculpture he created of her, and why did she ultimately destroy it? In the process of trying to find answers to these questions, I came across many other artists, both painters and photographers, who had created portraits of Klein throughout her long life. Although Melanie Klein was famously reticent about her personal life, guarded in conversation and in her writing and destroying many documents and virtually all the letters she received, there is a wealth of images of her, which, individually and collectively, provide an insight into her life, adding colour and nuance to the sparse literary narrative. These images also provide an opportunity to observe the convergence of often very different lives: how the portrait—the fruit of the brief creative collaboration between artist and psychoanalyst—is influenced by their life experiences, both shared and disparate. Melanie Klein struggled with the process of portraiture and was clearly ambivalent about the exposure this inevitably entailed, destroying two of the works of art created of her: a bust by Oscar Nemon and a painting by William Coldstream. Destroying a work of art is a powerful statement, which inevitably leads to a further question. Why were some of these creative collaborations successful and others not, or, to frame the question slightly differently, what was it the artists saw in Klein that she sometimes found so intolerable? For those who are unfamiliar with her, I hope this book will shine a sympathetic light on Melanie Klein's life and provide at least some answers to the many questions raised.

I have drawn on multiple sources during the research for this book, but I would first like to acknowledge my debt to Phyllis Grosskurth, whose biography of Klein, *Melanie Klein: Her World and Her Work* (1985), stands alone in the field. It is a pioneering examination of the Klein archives, a work of great scholarship and full of a surprising wealth of human detail, much of it provided by friends, colleagues, and relations who knew Klein personally and all of whom Phyllis Grosskurth was able to interview or communicate with directly. This is an invaluable source of information from those who bore witness to Klein's life, who knew her, who worked with her, and who in many cases loved her.

The Melanie Klein Trust has been consistently and enthusiastically helpful since the outset of this venture, and I am most grateful to the Trust for its unwavering encouragement and financial support. In particular, Dr John Steiner, a prominent contemporary Kleinian, has been generous and most stimulating in discussion, and many other psychoanalysts have also given freely of their time and thoughts, which have invariably been relevant, sometimes provocative, and always helpful. I would particularly wish to acknowledge in this regard my wife, Anne Amos, together with Jane Milton, Phil Crockett, and Helen Taylor-Robinson.

I would also like to extend special thanks to Melanie Klein's granddaughters, Diana Brimblecombe and Hazel Bentall, who were unfailingly kind and gracious and provided valuable insight into some of the images.

Sometimes the artist, particularly the photographer, is lost sight of in these encounters, but portraiture is a joint creative collaboration, and an understanding of the artist, his or her life and preoccupations, can only but illuminate our appreciation of the sitter. In this regard, I am particularly indebted to Lady Aurelia Young for her biography *Finding Nemon* (Young & Hale, 2018), about her father Oscar Nemon, and for generously providing much background information and many illustrations about her father's work and his relationship with Melanie Klein. I am also indebted to Bruce Laughton for his biography, *William Coldstream* (2004), and to Teresa Topolski, the daughter of Feliks Topolski, for information she provided about her father's drawings of Melanie Klein. I would also like to acknowledge the help and encouragement given by Philip Stokes, Christopher Glass, and Pierre Dupont.

It is a special pleasure to acknowledge the scholarship of Professor Janet Sayers, who has explored the relationship between William Coldstream, Adrian Stokes, and Melanie Klein with great insight and thoroughness, and I am indebted to her for an introduction to this world where art criticism and psychoanalysis meet.

Finally, I would like to extend my heartfelt thanks to the staff at the National Library of Scotland, who were helpful and efficient come what may and sourced without fuss many obscure references. I would also like to acknowledge the assistance of Luke Perry and Anna Irwin-Childs at the Institute of Psychoanalysis, who kindly provided the images of Oscar Nemon's low-relief sculptures of Melanie Klein.

It goes without saying that the opinions expressed are my own, unless acknowledged otherwise, and any errors or omissions are entirely mine.

ABOUT THE AUTHOR

Roger Amos is a retired doctor, in a previous life a haematologist working in the NHS in east London. His wife, Anne, is a psychoanalyst and a member of the British Psychoanalytical Society. He has lived on the fringes of the analytic world for many years, where Melanie Klein has been an abiding presence. This has been an opportunity to get to know her better.

CHAPTER ONE

Melanie Klein, portraits, and art

Melanie Klein [1882–1960] was Viennese, a woman with little formal education, trapped in an unhappy bourgeois marriage, who, through her own effort and determination, became an innovative and world-renowned psychoanalyst. An extraordinarily gifted and sensitive clinician, profound thinker, and tenacious intellectual, her radical ideas revolutionised the understanding of children's early development and made possible the treatment of psychotic patients, previously thought unavailable to psychoanalytic help. She began her life's work in the early years of the twentieth century, first in Budapest and then in Berlin, and by 1925 she had become pre-eminent in the psychoanalysis of children. To Klein, it is said, "is due the credit of carrying psycho-analysis to where it principally belongs—the heart of a child" (Jones, 1948, p. 338). Using play technique, she was able to explore the unconscious mind of the young child, which lead her to an understanding of the mental life of the baby and, in turn, to a clearer understanding of psychotic states of mind. Klein was devoted to her life's work, which she approached with commitment, courage, and integrity, working out the implications and consequences of her ideas with unshakeable honesty (Jones, 1955, p. 341). Perhaps partly because of this single-minded determination, throughout her life she was pursued by controversy, often vitriolic and venomous, and both she and her supporters had to fight long and hard to ensure the survival of her legacy. As Phyllis Grosskurth notes in her biography of Melanie Klein: "few professional women have been subjected to as much distilled malice and rumour accepted as fact as Klein endured both during her lifetime and since her death" (Grosskurth, 1985, p. x).

Attitudes towards Melanie Klein were highly charged and often deeply polarised, and the strength of feeling she generated, both then and now, is difficult to fully understand. Why this was so may be sought in her work, in which "the interior spaces of the psyche that she describes so literally both compel because they are revealed and appal because of what they reveal" (Stonebridge & Phillips, 1998, p. 3) or in her personality, which many of Klein's colleagues and friends struggled to describe. Hanna Segal put it thus:

> Mrs Klein as a person is not easy to describe. Like many creative people she was many-faceted, and accounts of her differ. She has been described by some as warm-hearted, tolerant and good-tempered; by others as intolerant, aggressive and demanding. She once described herself as primarily a very passionate person. [Segal, 1979, p. 170]

Many others were similarly conflicted, contrasting Klein's human warmth and sympathy with her steely determination and intellectual rigor. Partly, this was a consequence of the fact that she was "personally reticent to the point of secretiveness" (Jaques, 1983), carefully guarding the facts about her own personal life, leaving room for rumour and innuendo to flourish. She was said to have a "personality teeming with enthusiasm, intuitions and insights" (Likierman, 2001, p. 3), "full of human warmth, compassion and joie de vivre, vital and affectionate, feminine and quite coquettish, even in her old age" (Segal, 1979, p. 173)—someone, indeed, who "liked a good party, a good drink, a good laugh" (Pick & Milton, 2001, p. 6). But she was also a formidable champion of her theories and ideas, able to contemplate what to many seemed a "negative and pessimistic [view of] human nature" (Likierman, 2001, p. 4) through the utterly serious way in which she approached her work. She was tenacious and unforgiving in defence of the fundamental truths she believed she had discovered about human nature:

> Although she was tolerant, and could accept with an open mind the criticisms of her friends and ex-pupils, whom she often consulted, this was so only so long as one accepted the fundamental tenets of her work. If she felt this to be under attack, she could become very fierce in its defence. And if she did not get sufficient support from those she considered her friends, she could grow very bitter, sometimes in an unjust way. [Segal, 1979, pp. 170–171]

Criticism is never easy to accept, but for Klein disagreement or deviation perhaps sometimes felt like disloyalty, a betrayal of the cause to which she had dedicated her life. She was aware that the truths she had uncovered from her work with children were of unique importance, and, especially towards the end of her life, she was concerned for her psychoanalytic legacy, how to ensure the survival of her work:

> Within the limits of human capacity, I feel I have done something which perhaps in the future may prove to have been a great contribution to the understanding of the human mind . . . but I [have become] more and more doubtful whether my work will survive. . . . I have never been hopeless, nor am I now. It is a mixture of resignation and some hope that my work will perhaps after all survive and be of a great help to mankind. [Sayers & Forrester, 2013, pp. 153, 156]

Another important thread woven through Melanie Klein's personality, something that affected those around her and influenced their response to her, was her depression, hinted at in that excerpt from her autobiography. The source of this depression may be traced to the premature deaths of Klein's two siblings, her sister Sidonie when Klein was just 4 years old, and her brother Emanuel when she was 20 and on the verge of marriage. Melanie Klein herself believed that she never entirely recovered from these two deaths; about her sister, she said, "She died . . . when I was about 4½ and I have a feeling that I never entirely got over the feeling of grief for her death" (Sayers & Forrester, 2013, p. 139), and of her brother Emanuel: "The illness of my brother and his early death is another of the griefs in my life, which always remain alive in me" (Sayers

& Forrester, 2013, p. 141). For the rest of her life Klein regretted what her siblings might have achieved had they lived, and Hanna Segal was clear that these early traumas contributed to the lasting streak of depression, which she understood to be an integral part of Klein's personality (Segal, 1979, p. 30). The untimely deaths of her brother and sister were compounded by an unhappy marriage, at the age of just 21 and in the midst of grieving for her brother. Marriage meant the end of any further education or professional training, and Klein realised almost from the first that she was making a terrible mistake (Sayers & Forrester, 2013, p. 147). Melanie and Arthur Klein were married for twenty-four years and had three children together. During and after the pregnancies with her two sons, Hans and Eric, Klein was profoundly depressed, so much so that in 1909 she was admitted to a sanatorium for two and a half months of complete rest (Grosskurth, 1985, p. 56). Socially isolated, trapped in an unhappy marriage, and struggling with three young children, psychoanalysis was to provide Klein with escape and fulfilment. Perhaps not surprisingly, the premature death of her second analyst, Karl Abraham, her mentor and protector in Berlin, on Christmas Day 1925, and, much later, the shocking death of her son Hans in a walking accident in the Carpathian Mountains in 1934, both resulted in a profound crisis and a resurgence of the griefs and depression of the past. Despite the fact that "photographs have an inherent sadness, [appearing] to arrest time when in fact all they do, ultimately, is draw attention to its passing" (Dodd, 2014), many of the early images of Klein, those taken in her twenties and thirties, are characterised by an aura of melancholy and dejection. Perceptive observers continued to be aware of her depression, but, after the late 1930s, this is more hidden from casual view and becomes less and less apparent in the images made of her. Although it was partly an awareness of her own depression that had first brought her to psychoanalysis, "from the time she came to London it would have been very difficult to guess that" (Segal, 1979, pp. 172–173).

It is sometimes said that to take great photographs "you have to forgo judgment for empathy. You have to see yourself in your subject" (Carroll, 2015, p. 120). The extent to which the painters and sculptors who attempted to portray Klein identified with their subject and the aspects of her personality to which they related varied and was to prove a critical factor in the success or failure of the collaboration. Some of the artists, in particular William Coldstream, were intuitively in touch with Klein's profound sadness, a fact that proved to be very difficult for Klein, who reacted powerfully against his work. Others, especially some of the women artists, were able to find in Klein the mother they were each searching for in their different ways, and these were to be much more fruitful partnerships. Being a mother was difficult for Melanie Klein; her own mental distress, prolonged physical separations from her children, her psychoanalytic observations of their development, and the ultimate divorce of husband and wife all conspired against a fulfilling family life. The desire on Klein's part to be a good mother, to repair in some way the damage done to her children and family, was to find a positive outlet in her old age, expressed in her love for her grandchildren and in her nurturing of younger colleagues committed to her work (Grosskurth, 1985, p. 437; Quinodoz, 2013, p. 35) and, not least, in her creative relationships with some of the women artists who portrayed her.

∗ ∗ ∗

There are many possible answers to the question "Why portraiture?"— that unique, creative collaboration between artist and subject—but the fundamental response, whether it is a photograph, a painting, or a sculpture, is that portraiture is about commemoration: the portrait is an act of resistance against mortality. As the Renaissance scholar Leon Battista Alberti laconically observed, "through painting, the faces of the dead go on living for a very long time" (Fletcher, 2008, p. 46). But to commemorate, to bring someone back to remembrance, requires a "good likeness" in the broadest sense of the term, and this requirement for a good likeness means that portraiture is, by necessity, the most constrained of the arts. Whether the portrait is uncompromisingly realistic, a fleeting impressionistic study, or an abstracted form, the artist must create not only a recognisable physical likeness but also an insight into the inner essence of the subject. This requirement for a "good likeness" is the source of the tension that lies at the heart of portraiture, for what the artist "sees" and what the subject "wants" may be two very different things. How is the truth of the artist's vision—what the artist conceives to be the essential character lying beneath the mask and how to capture it most effectively—to be reconciled with the needs and wishes of the subject, how the subject wants to be seen and remembered by posterity? Working through this minefield of perception and expectation is the essential task that artist and subject must face together if the collaboration is to bear fruit.

Achieving a balance, reconciling these different perspectives, is no easy task, but when successful, it can be a very rewarding, even a moving, experience. Sara Lawrence-Lightfoot, a sociologist at Harvard University, recalls her experience of being painted, once as a child and again in her mid-twenties:

> These portraits did not capture me as I saw myself. . . . Instead they seemed to capture my essence—qualities of character and history some of which I was unaware of, some of which I resisted mightily, some of which felt deeply familiar. But the translation of image was anything but literal. It was probing, layered and interpretative. In addition to portraying my image, the piece expressed the perspective of the artist and was shaped by the evolving relationship between the artist and me. I also recognized that in searching for the essence, in moving beyond the surface image, the artist was both generous and tough, both skeptical and receptive. I was never treated or seen as an object, but always as a person of strength and vulnerability, beauty and imperfection, mystery and openness. [Lawrence-Lightfoot & Hoffman-Davis, 1997, p. 4]

Not all sitters subjected to intense artistic scrutiny are as generous and insightful as this, and not all artists are able to hold their subject in such a supportive way.

A portrait invariably comprises three distinct, but inseparable, realities: that of the sitter, the context, and, as the previous quotation makes clear, the artist him/herself. How is the artist to approach the task? Which of the many faces we present to the world—for there can be only one—will the artist choose to commemorate us by? How that choice is made and how the image is recreated in paint or stone reflects the artist's own sensibility, and the final portrait is not only an image of the subject but also, necessarily, a reflection of the artist him/herself. Always present in a portrait, the artist is vigilant and responsive but ideally never overwhelms the subject. Basil Hallward, who painted the famous picture of the beautiful young man Dorian Gray in the novel by Oscar Wilde, resolutely refused to exhibit the portrait to the public, because, he said:

> Every portrait that is painted with feeling is a portrait of the artist, not of the sitter. The sitter is merely an accident, the occasion. It is not he who is revealed by the painter; it is rather the painter, who, on the coloured canvas, reveals himself. The reason I will not exhibit this picture is that I am afraid that I have shown in it the secret of my soul. [Wilde, 1985, p. 9]

Although perhaps this overstates the case, for both partners in this collaboration the process of portraiture, whether sitting for a portrait or creating one, is an extraordinarily intimate experience. There are few occasions in adult life when we observe, often over a long period of time, a body and a face so closely, or allow such a prolonged, intense, and detailed scrutiny of ourselves. There are significant dangers here, not least that the subject may feel objectified or violated by the sublimated eroticism inherent in the artist's gaze. Mutual trust is therefore a key ingredient in this venture; artist and subject must each be able to rely fully on the honesty and integrity of the other. During the creation of any portrait worthy of the name, both artist and subject put themselves "on the line".

Figurative artists—photographers, sculptors, and painters—portrayed Melanie Klein on many occasions throughout her life, but she had a complicated relationship with them and with the process of portraiture itself. On the one hand, she was responsible for the destruction of two images of herself, a bust by the sculptor Oscar Nemon and a painting by William Coldstream; yet on the other, she collaborated with many photographers, who often produced very moving portraits of her. The remarkable series of portrait photographs that have come down to us trace Melanie Klein's life from a young child to an old lady—as sister, mother, and psychoanalyst. Although no single image can ever encompass the whole of an individual's character, and although these photographs reflect the norms and culture of the times, taken together they reveal with great candour the many facets of Klein's personality. In contrast to the paintings and sculptures, few in number and about which Klein's friends and colleagues held strong opinions, the photographic portraits of Klein, by turns romantic and wistful, sad and enigmatic, serious and uncompromising, seem to have generated little controversy, the very diversity of the images perhaps allowing each to choose the representation of Klein they feel most comfortable with. Despite her reservations about being painted or sculpted, Klein does not seem to have had the same qualms about being photographed. The gaze of the portrait artist is intense, prolonged, and potentially uncomfortable, and the delicate psychological engagement between artist and sitter requires considerable trust. In contrast, photography is more spontaneous, less considered, and over relatively quickly, and the artist's gaze is separated from the body of the sitter by the camera and bulk of the photographic apparatus, relieving the interaction of some at least of its intensity. It is perhaps these very differences that made it a more acceptable medium to Klein.

By all accounts, Klein "loathed" the bust created of her by the sculptor Oscar Nemon and ultimately destroyed it, having hid it in her attic for some years. She also insisted that work was stopped on a portrait of her by the artist William Coldstream, later demanding that it, too, should be destroyed. Putting to one side the ethics of destroying a work of art and the question of who, in fact, "owns" the image of an individual created by any artist, these destructive acts are powerful statements and beg the question: what drove Klein to such extreme ends? The only surviving figurative portraits of Klein are the recently discovered relief sculptures by Oscar Nemon and the portrait painting by Olga Dormandi—both serene, untroubled works, reflections of the warm, life-loving side of her character, aspects of herself that Klein found easiest to share with others. The works that did not survive, in particular the painting by William Coldstream, focused on aspects of herself that Klein found much more difficult to share; she recoiled from being brought face to face with those griefs from the past, refusing to be perpetuated in this way and denying any permanent triumph to the depression she had battled all her life. Klein is not alone in having sometimes found the experience of being portrayed a tormenting process and the outcome a persecution. Two anecdotes about Winston Churchill illustrate the problems that can arise.

The first concerns Churchill and the same sculptor, Oscar Nemon, who first met in 1951 in Marrakech, where Nemon had been invited for Christmas by his friend the French psychoanalyst René Laforgue. While sitting for the sculptor, Churchill reminded Nemon of an aphorism of the famous portraitist John Singer Sargent: "If you want to lose a friend, do his portrait." For his part, Nemon recalled, in his unpublished autobiography, how he struggled with a sitter who was "bellicose, challenging and deliberately provocative", trying to capture "not merely a likeness but a biography of his life", grappling with a subject of many moods "who [would] not surrender his personality to the artist as a sitter should" (Nemon, 2019). Churchill, always sensitive to the public perception of any image of himself, demanded "a portrait that would convey his features but make no statement; in short, a well-mannered and civilised portrait in the style of the Old Masters" (Young & Hale, 2018, p. 151).

The second anecdote is the well-known story of Graham Sutherland's portrait of Churchill (Jones, 2001). Graham Sutherland [1903–1980] was a leading modern romantic British artist, inspired by the Pembrokeshire coastline and most famous for his creation of the Coventry Cathedral tapestry. In 1954, to mark Churchill's 80th birthday, the House of Commons commissioned Sutherland to paint a portrait of the great man, who at that time was recovering from a stroke, which had been deliberately concealed from the public. Initially, all went well. Churchill's wife thought that Sutherland was "a most attractive man" and could "hardly believe that the savage and cruel designs which he exhibits come from his brush" (Soames, 1979, p. 488). Sutherland's portrait depicted Churchill as a magnificent ruin, hunched with age and dark in mood. Churchill took "an instant loathing to it", feeling betrayed that "this brilliant painter, with whom he had made friends while sitting for him, should see him as a gross and cruel monster" (Furness, 2015). His wife thought it was a "travesty of Winston, showing all the ravages of time and revealing nothing of the warmth and humanity of his nature" (Soames, 1979, p. 488). At the unveiling in Westminster Hall before a distinguished audience, Churchill was caustically sarcastic, and Sutherland was humiliated. The portrait was hidden from view at Chartwell, Churchill's home in Kent, and never publicly displayed. But there it came to prey upon Churchill's mind, so much so that his wife promised him "it would never see the light of day" (Soames, 1979, p. 549). She eventually conspired with her private secretary to have it burnt in the middle of the night. The painting's destruction was kept secret until after Lady Churchill's death in 1977; when the facts became known, many were horrified at the destruction of a work by such a distinguished artist, and for Sutherland himself it was simply an "act of vandalism" (Furness, 2015).

This story of Churchill and Sutherland has many similarities with the account of the portrait of Klein by the artist William Coldstream. They both powerfully illustrate the fundamental conflict at the root of portraiture between what the artist "sees" and what the subject "wants". They both also highlight the power of a mere image to torment an individual and expose the secrecy and shame that inevitably surrounds the destruction of a work of art.

* * *

Finally, one must also consider Melanie Klein's view of art in general and how this influenced her response to the artists who worked with her. Klein's appreciation of art, her attitude to art, was essentially a matter of the senses rather than the intellect, and this was to have a profound effect on how she responded to the portraits made of her. Klein enjoyed the theatre, opera, and painting, and she used art to illustrate her theories and ideas (Klein, 1929)—both an opera, *L'Enfant et les Sortilèges,* by Ravel, with a libretto by Colette, and the work of the Swedish artist Ruth Kjar (Segal, 1991, pp. 85–86). However, in Hanna Segal's opinion, papers such as this "dealt with points of psychological interest but not with the central problem of aesthetics, which is: what constitutes good art?" (Segal, 1998, p. 204). Richard Wollheim, the distinguished philosopher who, like his friend Adrian Stokes, used the principles of psychoanalysis in his work, wrote of Klein's attitude to painting:

> Mrs Klein did say to me once that she felt tremendous admiration for Adrian: she felt that there was something very rich and remarkable about him. But she said she didn't really understand a lot of his writing. As far as I could make out she had a very sensuous attitude to art, and I don't think that that really coincided with Adrian's. I think he was deeply absorbed and impressed by the notion of the struggle in the work of art: the struggle in making it, the struggle against the luxury of making it. [Read, 2002, p. 199]

William Coldstream shared with his friend Adrian Stokes that sense of struggle in the act of painting. But this struggle—the constant battle against a slide into easy sensuousness, the intellectual rigor and austerity of attitude necessary in all art, but perhaps especially in figurative art, if it is to be both honest and true—was not something that Klein engaged with or responded to with sympathy and understanding. Although she recognised William Coldstream's portrait of herself as potentially a great work of art, there was no warmth in her response to it—she just didn't like it. In contrast, she would treasure and ultimately bequeath to her family the painting of her by Olga Dormandi, distinguished from the Coldstream portrait by its generous colour, glowing sunlight, and warm humanity.

All agreed that Melanie Klein was an ideal subject for a portrait. Although small in stature, she was, according to Wilfred Bion, a "handsome, dignified and somewhat intimidating woman" (Abel-Hirsch, 2019, p. 124) with an imposing presence, commanding a room through the singular force of her personality. Many commented on her regal persona and, in particular, on her terrific head, with its large face and features and grand sweep of hair—a face, in fact, that demanded to be drawn, painted, or sculpted. It is a matter of great regret, therefore, that, despite her own remarkable creativity, Klein was unable to place her trust in the honesty and integrity of the two artists, Oscar Nemon and William Coldstream, who alone might have created a representation worthy of her commemoration. Despite her own and her friends' misgivings about their representations of her, there can be little doubt that either one would have enhanced, rather than detracted from, Klein's reputation and public persona. In the event, whether through anxiety about the security of her place in the analytic world or from a deeply held sense of her own lack of worth, Klein was unable to grasp this opportunity for commemoration and immortality.

CHAPTER TWO

Early life, childhood, and adolescence

Vienna, 1882 to 1902

M elanie Klein grew up in a Jewish family, emancipated from its orthodox past, with a tradition of learning and scholarship. Her father, Moriz Reizes [1828–1900], came from Lemburg (Lvov), in Galicia, of Polish parents, who were horrified when their son trained and qualified as a doctor, helping to look after the victims of a cholera epidemic in the Polish countryside and later practising as a physician in the small town of Deutsch-Kreutz (Burgenland). An arranged marriage in his youth had ended in divorce, and it was not until his mid-forties, on a visit to Vienna, that he met Libussa Deutsch [1852–1914], Melanie's mother. Twenty-four years younger than her future husband, Libussa came from a tight-knit, well-educated family in Warbotz (Verbotz), Slovakia. The couple married in 1875, and three children were born in quick succession, Emilie (1876), Emanuel (1877), and Sidonie (1878), with Melanie following, after a gap of four years, in 1882. Initially, the family continued to live in Deutsch-Kreutz, but they moved to Vienna some time before Melanie was born. When Melanie was about 5 years old, they were able to buy a flat in the Martinstrasse, in the comfortable middle-class suburb of Wahring, having inherited some money on the death of Moriz's father and with the financial help of his brother, Hermann.

The earliest-known portrait photograph of Melanie Reizes was taken in the Wimmer Studios in Vienna, in about 1888, shortly after the family's move to the Martinstrasse; it shows a 6-year-old Melanie with her two older siblings, Emanuel, aged 10, and Emilie, aged 11 (Figure 1). The children are carefully posed, the two girls in matching dresses and scuffed boots on either side of their brother, who takes centre stage. Emilie seems distracted, sullen perhaps, but Melanie and her brother are alert and attentive. Emanuel has a protective arm around his little sister's shoulder, whose "whole demeanor exhibits a remarkable self-assurance" (Grosskurth, 1985, p. 10). In her autobiography, Klein writes that she was about 9 years old when her deep friendship with Emanuel developed: "he was my confidant, my friend, my teacher" (Sayers & Forrester, 2013, p.140). Like many family photographs, it is what is not visible that is most significant. The missing presence is Sidonie, four years older than Melanie, who had died two years before this photograph was taken of scrofula (tuberculosis of the lymph glands in the neck); highly visible, repellent and a disease of the urban poor, "scrofulous" was a term of shame and abuse (Bynum, 2012, p. 32). Melanie idealised Sidonie and, much later in life, remembered her as "the best looking of us all" with "her violet-blue eyes, her black curls and her angelic face" (Sayers & Forrester, 2013, p. 139).

> Sidonie, lying in bed, took pity on me, and she taught me the principles of counting and of reading, which I picked up very quickly. It is quite possible that I idealize her a little, but my feeling is that, had she lived, we would have been the greatest of friends and I still have a feeling of gratitude to her for satisfying my mental needs, all the greater because I think she was very ill at the time. [Sayers & Forrester, 2013, p. 139]

Sidonie's death occurred a few years after Robert Koch had proved conclusively that tuberculosis was an infectious disease caused by the tubercle bacillus; but this understanding supplanted only gradually the long-held view that TB was in some way inheritable, the result of some familial weakness.

Figure 1   The Reizes children. Melanie, aged 6 (*c.*1888). Melanie is on the left, Emilie on the right, with Emanuel in the centre. *Unknown photographer, the Wimmer Studio, Vienna.* [*Copyright Melanie Klein Trust, reprinted with permission.*]

The frequency of multiple cases of pulmonary consumption in one household, and the extinction of many consumptive families, made it appear certain in the Northern countries that the disease was the outcome of a bad hereditary constitution. It was generally considered that little could be done for those born with a predisposition to phthisis beyond providing for them a climate and a way of life that would retard the inexorable course of their disease. [Dubos & Dubos, 1996, pp. 42–43]

Emanuel also had TB, possibly contracted from his little sister, and he was to die in 1902, aged 25, of a combination of TB and severe rheumatic heart disease (Grosskurth, 1985, p. 17), the latter a direct consequence of an attack of scarlet fever occurring shortly after this photograph was taken. Emanuel's mother, Libussa, seems to have blamed herself for her son's heart ailments, because she had insisted that he accompany the family on a trip to the Prater (a popular amusement park in Vienna) while he was still convalescing from scarlet fever. Although never spoken of, it was always understood within the family, and by Emanuel himself, that "he could not live longer than some time in his twenties" (Sayers & Forrester, 2013, p. 142). Tuberculosis and the possibility of premature death must have haunted the family as the children were growing up (Sherwin-White, 2017, p. 10). Much later the two surviving sisters, Emilie and Melanie, remained fearful of the disease; when Emilie was diagnosed with lung cancer in 1940, she apparently made the doctors swear to her that she did not in fact have tuberculosis, and it is possible that one of the reasons Melanie never visited her sister during her final illness was because of her long-standing dread of tuberculosis (Grosskurth, 1985, p. 250).

Two years later, when Melanie was 8, she was photographed at the Olga Studios in Vienna, where her mother had also been photographed when she was a young woman. This time on her own, Melanie is confident, smiling, bright-eyed, and vivacious (Figures 2 & 3). Wearing a pale, lacy dress and holding trailing flowers and foliage in her lap, with earrings and long, luxuriant hair, she engages self-confidently with the photographer. As with the earlier family group, there is no information about who the particular photographer was,

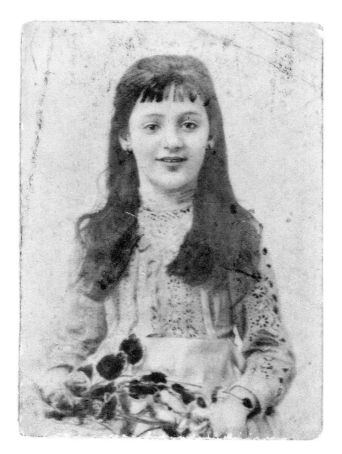

Figure 2 Melanie Klein, aged 8 (c.1890). *Unknown photographer, the Olga Studio, Vienna. [Copyright Melanie Klein Trust, reprinted with permission.]*

but he or she was clearly able to establish an easy rapport with the young Melanie. Both the Wimmer and Olga studios were in Alsenstrasse, close to the flat where the family lived and in the same street where Melanie went to school. Melanie was an ambitious student from the youngest age. She greatly admired what she saw as the immense learning of her father, and he, in his turn, was very proud of the academic achievements of his youngest daughter. Her greatest pride was to receive a school report with the words *wurde belobt* (commended) written on it (Grosskurth, 1985, p. 9).

Figure 3 Melanie Klein, aged 8 (c.1890). *Unknown photographer, the Olga Studio, Vienna. [Copyright Melanie Klein Trust, reprinted with permission.]*

The next sequence of six portrait photographs (Figures 4 to 9) were taken when Melanie was aged between 16 and 20, in the studios of Carl Pietzner [1853–1927], a prominent Viennese society photographer, who had many members of the Austro-Hungarian royal family among his clientele. Pietzner started work in a photographic studio in Wriezen, Brandenburg, as a young man in 1864, and, because of his skills as a retoucher, subsequently travelled widely—to Berlin, St Petersburg, and Moscow. He was appointed photographer to the Hapsburg Court in 1893 and opened his first studio in Vienna in

Figure 4 Melanie Klein, aged 16 (c.1898). *Unknown photographer, the Carl Pietzner Studio, Vienna. [Copyright Melanie Klein Trust, reprinted with permission.]*

1895; subsequently, his business came to dominate the portrait photographic market there, expanding throughout the Austro-Hungarian Empire as well as to the two principal cities of Russia. In the early 1900s, his was one of the largest studios. He was among the most sought-after photographers in Vienna, with ten studios in the city and employing over 300 staff. Despite this commercial success, either he or his son indulged in high-risk financial speculation during the First World War, resulting in severe financial difficulties for the business and ultimately in Carl Pietzner's suicide.

Figure 5   Melanie Klein, aged 18 (1900). *Unknown photographer; the Carl Pietzner Studio, Vienna. [Copyright Melanie Klein Trust, reprinted with permission.]*

20

Figure 6   Melanie Klein, aged 18 (c.1900). *Unknown photographer, the Carl Pietzner Studio, Vienna. [Copyright Melanie Klein Trust, reprinted with permission.]*

This series of photographs, stylistically all very similar, catch the transition between childhood and early womanhood. In the earliest portrait, from 1898, Melanie is a slightly gauche-looking 16-year-old photographed in half profile, wearing a sleeveless white dress; her hair is unruly, but the full lips and heavy-lidded eyes are already apparent. Then, as we watch, in the space of a few years, she matures into a demure, beautiful young woman; there are no smiles, the eyes are hooded, the long hair is drawn back and elaborately pinned, she is poised and elegant, and, in the full-face portrait, the gaze is direct and open. In the words of her biographer, she is "a voluptuous dark

Figure 7   Melanie Klein, aged 20 (*c.*1902). *Unknown photographer, the Carl Pietzner Studio, Vienna.* [*Copyright Melanie Klein Trust, reprinted with permission.*]

beauty with heavy lidded eyes . . . aware of her desirability as all her brother's friends seemed to be falling in love with her" (Grosskurth, 1985, p. 19).

Although dismissed later in life by her detractors as "an uneducated woman" (Grosskurth, 1985, p. 14), Melanie Klein was not only beautiful, but also highly intelligent; mocked by her siblings for her precocity (Grosskurth, 1985, p. 14), she excelled at the *lyceum*, passing the entrance examinations for the *gymnasium* aged 16, in 1898. Even at this young age she had already expressed her wish to study medi-

Figure 8   Melanie Klein, aged 20 (c.1902). *Unknown photographer, the Carl Pietzner Studio, Vienna. [Copyright Melanie Klein Trust, reprinted with permission.]*

cine, like her father and brother Emanuel before her—a brave and radical ambition on the part of a woman in Vienna at the turn of the century. The university had only begun to admit women in 1897, and then only to study philosophy; women were not to be admitted to the medical school until three years later (Sherwin-White, 2017, p. 11). Despite these bold intentions, in 1899, aged just 17, Melanie met and in 1901 was formally engaged to her future husband, Arthur Klein, a commitment that ended all prospects of further education and of an independent professional career. All her life Klein regretted not having

Figure 9   Melanie Klein, aged 20 (*c.*1902). *Unknown photographer, the Carl Pietzner Studio, Vienna. [Copyright Melanie Klein Trust, reprinted with permission.]*

studied medicine, believing, according to Hanna Segal, "that if she had had a medical degree her views would have been listened to with more respect" (Segal, 1979, p. 31).

Arthur Klein [1878–1939] was an ambitious, serious young man (Figure 10), studying to be an industrial chemist at the prestigious Swiss Federal Technical High School in Zurich, a distant relative of Melanie's, as well as a friend of and greatly admired by her brother Emanuel. Whether or not the family's financial circumstances were a factor in the decision to become engaged is unclear (Sayers & Forrester, 2013, p. 157),

Figure 10 Arthur Klein, aged 18 (1896); taken three years before he met Melanie, in 1899. *Unknown photographer, Zurich.* [*Copyright Melanie Klein Trust, reprinted with permission.*]

but in her autobiography Klein claims to have known even then that she was making a dreadful mistake:

> From that time I was so loyal that I refrained from any entertainment where I might have met other young men and never expressed a feeling that I already had in my mind, that we were not really suited to one another. . . . I was already deeply disappointed [but] [b]oth loyalty to my fiancé, with whom I was up to a point in love, and circumstances prevented me from mentioning this to my mother or my brother. [Sayers & Forrester, 2013, pp. 147, 157]

Figure 11   Dr Arthur Klein, aged 24 (1902); taken in Boston just before he left America to return to Europe, the year before his marriage. *Unknown photographer, Boston, Massachusetts.* [*Copyright Melanie Klein Trust, reprinted with permission.*]

Much of the time after they first met until their marriage four years later the couple spent apart, with Arthur completing his training in America, while Melanie spent long periods of time with her future in-laws in Rosenberg (Ruzomberok), in northern Slovakia. In September 1902, appearing mature beyond his years and now with a doctorate (Figure 11), Arthur Klein returned to Vienna from Boston with the prospect of a job in the paper mill in Rosenberg, and plans for the marriage went ahead. During Melanie and Arthur's engagement it became clear that Emanuel was dying, transformed from a fresh-

Figure 20 Melanie Klein, aged 28 (c.1910). *Unknown photographer, Budapest.* [*Copyright Melanie Klein Trust, reprinted with permission.*]

from the foreboding, oppressive atmosphere and sense of entrapment that characterise the previous portraits. One shows Klein in almost full profile (Figure 21), and the other has her wearing an elegant hat (Figure 22). The images may have been captured by János Szabó, although there is no other information about the photographer. The second image, the one with Klein wearing a hat, is noteworthy for the slight tilt of the head, sideways glance, and modest elevation of the eyebrows, features that give a questioning, slightly quizzical expression, as if Klein were gently

Figure 21   Melanie Klein, aged 29 (c.1911). *Possibly taken by János Szabó, Budapest.* [*Copyright Melanie Klein Trust, reprinted with permission.*]

interrogating the photographer—a look that can often be recognised in subsequent portraits. Shortly after these photographs were taken, and somewhat belying their conventionality, Klein began work on a series of semi-autobiographical poems, short stories, and prose fragments, which occupied her for the next seven years, from 1913 to 1920, and which explored "the longing of a woman for a richer and fuller life, particularly for sexual gratification, and the conflict that is stirred up by these forbidden wishes" (Grosskurth, 1985, p. 64). Many of the stories barely conceal "her hostility towards Arthur", her husband (Grosskurth, 1985, p. 69),

Figure 22   Melanie Klein, aged 29 (c.1911).   *Possibly taken by János Szabó, Budapest.*
[*Copyright Melanie Klein Trust, reprinted with permission.*]

Figure 23 Melanie Klein, aged 30 (c.1912–13). *Aladár Székely , Budapest.* [*Copyright Melanie Klein Trust, reprinted with permission.*]

although, as Grosskurth writes, "they are never embarrassing and they never ring false" and can be admired for "their absolute sincerity, their soul-searching honesty and the genuine expression of a tortured mind" (Grosskurth, quoting Bruni Schling, 1985, p. 66).

The final image from Budapest (Figure 23), like many of the previous ones, is not accurately dated but was taken sometime when Klein was in her early thirties. Her third child, Eric, was born in July 1914, after another period of pregnancy-associated depression, made worse by the death of her mother in November, shortly after the birth.

Melanie had nursed her mother during her last, short illness, and Hanna Segal recalled that Melanie was "deeply moved by the serenity and courage with which her mother approached death . . . and often spoke of it in her old age" (Segal, 1979, p. 28). In 1958, shortly before her own death, Klein recalled, when sympathising with a colleague, Marcelle Spira, whose own mother had just died, "My mother's death has caused me great pain and it took me some time to get over the depression which followed. How often do I think about her even now and miss her—in some ways she remained alive with me!" (in Quinodoz, 2015, p. 98).

For the first time there is some biographical information about the artist who captured the image. Aladár Székely [1870–1940] was born in Gyula, in the south-east of Hungary close to the Romanian border, the second oldest of seven children (Figure 24). The family changed their surname from Bleyer to Székely sometime during Aladár's childhood to make them sound and appear more Hungarian. A poor scholar, Székely's artistic skills led to his apprenticeship with the Dunky brothers, Kálmán and Ferenc, pioneer Hungarian photographers, and Székely opened his first independent photographic studio in Budapest in 1899. A gentle man with frail health, he became a renowned photographer who captured images of many of the most important cultural figures in Hungary during the first decades of the twentieth century, including Sándor Ferenczi, Klein's first analyst, and Endre Ady, Hungary's most famous lyric poet [1877–1919], who was also a well-known politically active journalist with a resolute belief in social progress. Székely adored his poet friend, and Endre's premature death in 1919 left the photographer devastated. He afterwards retreated, leaving the world behind and spending long periods of time in his silent studio, producing very little work.

Székely's stated aim was for truth and realism, and his approach to photography was revolutionary in its simplicity; his photographic portraits are uncluttered, and he worked quickly to catch character. He used only natural light and was particularly concerned with modelling the face and hands, the two aspects of his subjects that he felt were most sensitive to the sitter's character. The innovative and uncompromising

Figure 24   Aladár Székely (date unknown). *Unknown photographer.*

nature of his work was recognised by Endre, his poet friend, who wrote in the preface to a book of Székely's portrait photographs, *Writers and Artists*, published in 1915,

> Of course, these realistic photographs are not for everyone's liking—one likes to see his neighbour more like himself—but still more people are beginning to appreciate the unbearableness of Aladár Székely's artistic honesty. [Székely, 2019]

Aladár married in in 1905, and his only son, László, was born in 1910, probably shortly before the portrait photograph of Klein was taken; he took over his father's business sometime in the 1930s. Székely himself died in 1940 at the beginning of the Second World War; during the war, the studio in Budapest was bombed, and many of Székely's photographic negatives were damaged or destroyed. László was killed while fighting with the Axis troops at the battle for the liberation of Voronezh in 1943, when the strategic city on the river Don was recaptured from the German invaders by the Red Army. The death of his son and the destruction of his studio meant that Székely 's reputation was eclipsed after his death, and only recently has his groundbreaking originality been re-discovered and his reputation restored.

In Székely's remarkable image (Figure 23), which perhaps encapsulates her time in Budapest, Klein is pictured alone and vulnerable, in a bleak and claustrophobic landscape. Her dress is black, austere, and unadorned, and the viewer's gaze is drawn to the bare, dazzlingly white skin. The features of the face, which are beautifully defined by the subtle lighting, are sad and downcast; the eyes are averted, refusing to engage either with the photographer or with us. When trying to make sense of this haunting image, it helps to remember that by now both Klein's parents are dead, as are her two most cherished siblings; she is trapped in a marriage that, by her own admission, she realised almost from the start was a dreadful mistake, and she is struggling to bring up three young children. Psychoanalysis was to offer Klein a way out of this personal cul-de-sac and ultimately provide her with liberation and fulfilment.

CHAPTER FOUR

The unrecorded decade

Budapest and Berlin, 1914 to 1925

The Hungarian Psychoanalytical Society was formally constituted in 1913, and, despite the outbreak of war and the fact that Sándor Ferenczi was called up to serve as a doctor in the Hungarian Army, psychoanalytic life continued in Budapest. In September 1918, the 5th International Psychoanalytical Association Congress was held in the city, to great acclaim, and Ferenczi was elected president. This Congress was the first occasion when Melanie Klein saw Freud, and she recalled later that "I remember vividly how impressed I was and how the wish to devote myself to psycho-analysis was strengthened" (Sayers & Forrester, 2013, p. 149). It was Ferenczi who had first drawn Klein's attention to her gift for understanding children and suggested to her that she pursue her interest in child analysis, and in July 1919 Klein presented her first paper to the Hungarian Society about a child analysis, following which she was awarded full membership of the society.

But this intellectual idyll could not last. Following the shattering defeat of the Hapsburg Empire in the First World War, political turmoil overwhelmed Hungary. A brief Bolshevik regime, led by Béla Kun, was overthrown by Horthy's right-wing nationalists, who instituted a virulent anti-Semitic pogrom, *The White Terror*. Life became very difficult for professional Jews in general, and for Hungarian psychoanalysts in particular. Political humiliation was total; at the Treaty of Trianon, in 1920, Hungary lost two-thirds of its territory and over half of its population. The problems in Klein's personal life came to a crisis at the same time. Arthur Klein had been called up to serve in the Austro-Hungarian army in late 1914 but was invalided out with a leg wound two years later. As the political situation deteriorated, he could no longer continue in his managerial post, and in 1919 he moved to Sweden for employment. Melanie, with their three children, went again to stay with her in-laws in Rosenberg, marking the beginning of a four-year separation from her husband. In 1921, at least in part due to the rabid anti-Semitism in Hungary, Klein moved to Berlin with her youngest son, Eric, then aged 8, Hans went to live with his father, and Melitta stayed in Rosenberg to study and matriculate, later joining her mother in Berlin and enrolling as a medical student at the university there. Although the five years she lived in Berlin were a very creative period for Klein, it was also a very difficult time in her life, domestically, financially, and emotionally, and this is perhaps why few pictures or portraits have come down to us from these turbulent years. Perhaps none survived the vicissitudes of the times, or possibly Klein was too preoccupied with her career and family to be bothered. But standing in front of a camera requires a certain self-confidence; tentatively starting out in her chosen profession, with no clarity in her personal life, perhaps Klein just felt unable to face the scrutiny of an artist.

Arthur Klein rejoined his family, moving to Berlin in 1923, and the couple attempted a reconciliation. They built a house in the affluent and fashionable suburb of Dahlem, and for the first time in a long while the family were together again, all under one roof. But old patterns of behaviour soon re-emerged. Arthur, rigidly inflexible and strong-willed (Grosskurth, 1985, p. 19), attempted to impose his will on the household. He bullied Hans, he took a dislike to Melitta's suitor, Walter Schmideberg, and he was disapproving and antagonistic towards psychoanalysis and to what he saw as its damaging effects on his children

(Grosskurth, 1985, p. 110). Shortly after Melitta and Walter married, in April 1924, Melanie moved out, taking her youngest son with her; the couple were formally divorced two years later. Despite this domestic turmoil, Klein entered enthusiastically into the somewhat frenzied social and cultural life of post-war Berlin, going to concerts, the opera, and numerous balls—determined, in the words of Alix Strachey, "to have a thousand adventures" (Grosskurth, 1985, p. 133). It was at one of these dances that she met Chezkel Zvi Kloetzel [1891–1951], a journalist on the *Berliner Tageblatt*, nine years younger than Klein and already married, with a daughter. A brief, passionate affair ensued, from early spring 1925 until late summer the same year, when it was ruthlessly terminated by Kloetzel.

In Berlin Klein continued the work with child patients that she had begun in Budapest, and shortly after her arrival she met Nelly Wollfheim, a child therapist who ran a kindergarten. Wollfheim later wrote that she was "dumbfounded by the pretty, intelligent and confident creature sitting bolt upright on the sofa talking non-stop about her views on child psychology" (Grosskurth, 1985, p. 119). Klein almost certainly met Freud face to face at the 7th International Congress held in Berlin in 1922, the last congress he attended in person. She took the opportunity to present her ideas about childhood anxiety to him but was bitterly disappointed that he seemed not to be listening, his mind elsewhere (Grosskurth, 1985, p. 126). The president of the Berlin Psychoanalytical Society at this time was Karl Abraham, who was, in Michael Balint's words, "the very best president I ever met in my life. He was simply magnificent, fair and absolutely firm" (Grosskurth, 1985, p. 123). It was Karl Abraham who provided Klein with the protective nurturing environment in which she could develop, present, and discuss her work. Klein was made a full member of the Berlin Society in 1923; shortly afterwards, in early 1924, she entered analysis with Abraham.

The only portrait of Klein to survive from these years is a brief sketch by Róbert Berény [1887–1953], an avant-garde painter who had learnt his art in Paris, where he was strongly influenced by Cézanne; he later introduced cubism and expressionism to his native Hungary. Berény

Figure 25   Melanie Klein, aged 42 (1924). *Róbert Berény, drawn at the 8th International Psychoanalytical Congress, Salzburg, 1924. [Copyright Granger Historical Picture Archive/ Alamy Stock Photos.]*

was the teacher of Olga Dormandi, another Hungarian artist, who was to paint Klein in the 1940s and whose family formed the nucleus of the Budapest analytic world. Teacher and pupil collaborated on a series of caricatures of leading psychoanalysts who attended the 8th International Psychoanalytical Congress in Salzburg in 1924. In this rapid drawing, Klein is caught in austere profile (Figure 25). Like many caricatures, it is not flattering, but the drawn-back hair and the hooded eyes are familiar. The chin is exaggerated and powerful, the neck thick and bull-like, and the bosom expansive. One might speculate that the artist, and perhaps her colleagues also, were discovering that Klein was a formidable and ambitious woman.

Later that same year, in December 1924, Klein travelled to Vienna to present a paper on child analysis to the Vienna Psychoanalytic Society. "If Melanie Klein showed courage in discussing her theories before a sceptical Berlin audience she was a veritable Daniel entering the lion's den in daring to address the Viennese" (Grosskurth, 1985, p. 126). Klein does not write about the visit in her autobiography, but it was clearly a difficult and humiliating experience, not least because the Freuds failed to see her socially, even though Walter Schmideberg, by this time Melanie's son-in-law, was a close friend of the Freud family and a frequent visitor to their house on Berggasse. Ignored and ostracised by Freud, Klein was also an outsider in the Berlin Society (Grosskurth, 1985, p. 121). Her father's origins from Poland placed her low on the scale of the rigid Jewish social hierarchy, and in the highly intellectual environment in Berlin she was the only child analyst and was also neither an academic nor a doctor. Michael Balint remembered:

> Time and again she brought her clinical material, using very coura-geously and for the sake of greater faithfulness the naïve expressions of the nursery as her child patients did, often causing in her learned and reluctant audience embarrassment, incredulity or even sardonic laughter. [Balint, 1952, p. 214]

Like Klein, Michael Balint, together with his wife Alice and many other Hungarian analysts, had also left Budapest in 1921 to escape the flood-tide of anti-Semitism. Among this group were Sándor Radó and Franz Alexander, the two psychoanalysts who were to become the most vehe-ment of Klein's critics in Berlin. The murder in 1924 of Hermine Hug-Hellmuth, the director of the Child Guidance Centre in Vienna, by her patient, who was also her nephew, and, in late 1925, the sudden illness and premature death of Karl Abraham, left Klein exposed, vulnerable to open, savage criticism, led by her two compatriot Hungarian analysts. Feeling attacked by her colleagues in Berlin, without the protection pre-viously afforded by Abraham, and encouraged by Ernest Jones, in 1926 Klein left Berlin for good to live and work in London, her youngest son Eric joining her three months later. Arthur and Melanie Klein's divorce was finally formalised in the same year. The move to London was a brave "throw of the dice"—an attempt to find somewhere she could build a new life in an environment and among colleagues conducive to her ideas and work.

CHAPTER FIVE

Middle years

London, 1926 to 1950

Klein arrived to live permanently in London in September 1926, but in July of the previous year she had presented a series of lectures to the embryonic British Psychoanalytical Society. Despite initial anxieties about her ability to deliver them in English, the lectures were, by all accounts, well received by an interested and appreciative audience. The enthusiastic reception of these lectures was an important factor in Klein's decision to make the fateful move to London. But establishing herself there would not be easy: her personal situation as a divorced mother of three was unusual, to say the least; professionally she was without any formal education or medical qualification; and she was known to be out of favour with Freud and his daughter Anna and also to have antagonised her colleagues in Berlin.

Shortly after arriving in London, Klein was photographed by Herbert Lambert; this was the first time she had sat for a portrait photograph since the haunting image captured by Aladár Székely some ten years previously. Herbert Lambert [1882–1936] had recently been appointed head of the long-established Victorian photographic studio, Elliot and Fry's (Figure 26). Lambert was a Quaker, imprisoned as a conscientious objector during the Great War; intense, elegant, and

Figure 26   Herbert Lambert in his mid-40s (late 1920s). *Self-portrait.* [*Copyright The National Portrait Gallery, London, reprinted with permission.*]

sophisticated, he was also an accomplished musician who not only played the harpsichord and clavichord, but also built and repaired the instruments (Figure 27). As a portrait photographer, he specialised in images of composers and musicians, with whom he had a particular empathy, and in 1923 he published a celebrated book, *Modern British Composers: Seventeen Portraits,* featuring portraits of well-known musicians, documenting and celebrating the renaissance of British music in the early years of the twentieth century. In 1927 Lambert lent a clavichord he had made to the young composer Herbert Howells; in gratitude to Lambert for opening his eyes to the expressive qualities of the instrument, Howells named his Opus 41, a set of twelve pieces for clavichord, *Lambert's Clavichord.*

Herbert Lambert was a master at tightly controlling the studio lighting, which he understood to be the key "to modeling the head to bring out its true and essential form and to ensure that the final portrait was a sensitive rendering of the inner nature of the subject" (Lambert, 1930, p. 6). In his view, "the final print must be a thing of beauty in itself" (Lambert, 1930, pp. 6–7). What we see in Herbert Lambert's portraits is exactly what he wanted us to see. He had no time for extraneous props and thought the tendency of the early portrait studios "to be cumbered

Figure 27   Herbert Lambert, aged 47 (1929); Lambert is at work repairing a harpsichord. *F & B Goodwin. [Copyright The National Portrait Gallery, London, reprinted with permission.]*

with pillars, pedestals and curtains" and "painted back-cloths mimicking some of the most conventional features of the Grand Style" (Lambert, 1930, p. 12) to be particularly unfortunate.

Professionally, this early period in London was a productive one for Klein, despite the fact that March 1927 was the occasion when Klein's views on child analysis were openly ridiculed and repudiated by Anna Freud at a meeting of the Berlin Psychoanalytical Society (Sherwin-White, 2017, p. 30). Lambert's portrait of Klein (Figure 28), taken in the same year, 1927, is a complete contrast to the last image of her captured by Székely in Budapest. Anything but vulnerable, Klein now appears formidable and emanates a new self-confidence. Lambert has chosen to emphasise Klein's exotic foreignness, her central European origins—an impression conveyed perhaps by the swathes of fur framing the face and the white blouse, which gives an almost judicial feel to the picture. The portrait is dramatically lit but cold, and perhaps most unsettling of all is Klein's unflinching gaze, directed straight at the photographer and straight at us. This is a new and disturbing innovation in the portraits of Klein. Lambert's portrait is an almost brutal depiction of what he saw as Klein's determination and resolution.

* * *

The first serious attempt to portray Klein other than by photography was by the Croatian sculptor Oscar Nemon (born Oskar Neumann), in the uneasy spring of 1939, on the eve of the Second World War. At the time, Nemon was 32 years old, a sculptor with an established reputation on the continent but virtually unknown in England, where he had arrived shortly before, another refugee fleeing Nazi persecution in Europe.

Oscar Nemon [1906–1985] was born in Osijek, a small town in Croatia on the fringes of the Austro-Hungarian Empire. Although he always remembered his childhood as happy, his father had died of tuberculosis when he was just 9 years old, instilling in him an understanding of the fragility of family happiness (Young & Hale, 2018, p. 19). At school he was known as a shy and reclusive boy (Young & Hale, 2018, p. 21). Self-taught, with no formal artistic education (Young & Hale, 2018, p. 25), his precocious talent was recognised when he was very young, and he

Figure 28   Melanie Klein, aged 45 (1927). *Herbert Lambert, Elliot and Fry's Studio, London. [Copyright Melanie Klein Trust, reprinted with permission.]*

55

was advised, by the renowned Croatian sculptor Ivan Meštrović, to go to Paris and "find himself" (Young & Hale, 2018, p. 26). But, in the event, in September 1924, aged just 18, Nemon travelled to Vienna and immersed himself in the vibrant artistic life of the city, meeting the expressionist painter Oskar Kokoschka, sculpting a head of Richard Strauss, and attending concerts of Mahler's music. He came, however, to find the atmosphere in the city intolerable, particularly the hostility of the Viennese to the experimental art of the time, coupled with what he described as an all-pervading atmosphere of despair, misery, and degradation (Young & Hale, 2018, p. 36). He was particularly distressed by a meeting with a rich art collector, a possible subject for a sculpture, who explained that Nemon was too late—he was bankrupt: "I'm just deliberating what to do. I've nothing left except that revolver, and it could well be the solution to all my problems" (Young & Hale, 2018, p. 36). Carl Pietzner, whose studios had documented Klein's youth and adolescence, was not alone; many in post-war Vienna had been brought to financial ruin. After Nemon's rejection by the Vienna Art Academy, which operated a Jewish quota system, the young, fiercely ambitious sculptor left Vienna for Brussels, where he trained at the Académie Royale des Beaux-Arts and in time established himself as a leading European portrait sculptor (Nemon, 2019). It was in Brussels that he changed his birth name Neumann to Nemon, Oskar having become Oscar some years earlier. Gentle and witty, with a soft, accented voice, he was magically charming (Young & Hale, 2018, p. 78); when he walked into a room, it was "as if he came straight out of a gothic cathedral", with great hypnotic eyes and a subtle smile (Young & Hale, 2018, p. 118). Early on in his career, Nemon experienced at first hand the perennial conflict inherent in portraiture between the wishes of the subject and the vision of the artist. In 1926, he was commissioned to make a medallion portrait of Dr Ante Aksamovich, the Catholic Bishop of Djakovo. The Bishop was not happy with the result, complaining that Nemon had made him look like "a brute and a Turk" and demanding that the sculptor soften the hard lines of the relief; unsurprisingly, Nemon refused (Young & Hale, 2018, p. 44).

Nemon had a lifelong interest in psychoanalysis and, over the years, sculpted many famous practitioners, including Sándor Ferenczi (in

Figure 29   Oscar Nemon and Sigmund Freud (1931). *Unknown photographer, Vienna.* [*Copyright the Oscar Nemon Estate, with the kind permission of Aurelia Young.*]

1931), Marie Bonaparte (in 1937), Ernest Jones (in 1936), Abraham Brill (date unknown), Paul Federn (in 1949), René Laforgue (in the 1930s), and Donald Winnicott (in the 1960s); but his most illustrious subject, and one he returned to again and again, was Sigmund Freud. While in Vienna as a young man of 19, Nemon had approached Paul Federn, an early supporter and colleague of Freud, with a request to sculpt the great man. Freud refused the presumptuous, unknown artist; but in 1931 Nemon was summoned back to Vienna by Federn, who had secured provisional agreement for a sculpture to commemorate Freud's 75th birthday. Freud had apparently agreed only to meet, not to sit for the sculptor, and Nemon recounts in his unpublished autobiography the difficult initial meeting:

> I was duly admitted to the famous consulting room in his summer residence outside Vienna. Professor Freud stood up behind his desk, I bowed to him, our eyes met and he said sharply "Dr Federn said that you wanted to see me, well you have seen me!" I knew nothing of the exchange between Federn and Freud that had precipitated this remark and, at that time, filled with the indomitable pride of youth, felt rather

insulted and said "No sir, I have not seen you." [Young & Hale, 2018, p. 62]

Despite this fraught start, the brief sittings between patients progressed well, although Nemon found his subject reserved and uncommunicative (Figure 29). Freud praised the work in progress in a letter to Max Eitingon in August 1931:

> Someone is making a bust of me, the sculptor Oscar Neumann from Brussels, from his appearance a Slavic, eastern Jew, Khazar or Kalmuck or something like that. Federn, who is usually highly inept in discovering unacclaimed geniuses, forced him on me. But this time there is

Figure 30 Oscar Nemon and his statue of Freud (1969). *Falcon Stuart (Oscar Nemon's son).* [*Copyright Oscar Nemon Estate, with the kind permission of Aurelia Young.*]

something or rather quite a lot in it. The head, which the gaunt, goatee-bearded artist has fashioned from the dirt—like the good Lord—is a very good and an astonishingly life-like impression of me. [Molnar, 1992, p. 100]

In October 1931, the Vienna Psychoanalytic Society presented Freud with three busts by Nemon, one in wood, one in bronze, and the other in stone. Freud eventually chose to keep the wooden head, which, as he put it in a letter to Federn in November, "with its lively and friendly expression promises to be a pleasant room companion" (Molnar, 1992, p. 111). The head sat in his consulting room in Vienna, travelled to London with him seven years later, and is now in the Freud Museum in Hampstead. Paula Fichtl, Freud's housekeeper, thought it made Freud look too angry, to which Freud is said to have famously replied, "But I am angry. I am angry with humanity" (Molnar, 1992, p. 100). This marked the beginning of a fruitful association between Freud and the sculptor. Nemon would visit Freud in Vienna, en route between Brussels and Croatia, when he would sketch and mould further clay heads. They met for the last time in 1938, both refugees, having arrived in London at almost the same time. It is these later sittings that ultimately resulted in the harsher, more troubled head used in the full-sized, seated bronze statue of Freud unveiled in October 1970 and placed, in 1998, outside the Tavistock Clinic in Hampstead (Figure 30). A bronze replica was installed on the campus of the Medical University of Vienna in 2018, to commemorate the eighty years since Freud was forced to flee his home city (Young & Hale, 2018, p. 72).

During his early years in London, Nemon was preoccupied with his rather grandiose plans to build a Temple of Universal Ethics, a building to symbolise "the moral unification of all nations, creeds and races"—his response as a sculptor to the "desperate circumstances, which confront mankind today". The project, a consolation and distraction, ultimately came to nothing (Wood, 2015, p. 13). Much later, in 1965, "Humanity", his memorial commemorating the victims of the Holocaust and dedicated to the local Jewish community, was finally unveiled in the main square of Osijek, Nemon's home in Croatia, a city where 90% of the Jewish population perished, including his mother, grandmother, brother, and most of his extended family, denounced by their neighbours and murdered at the hands of the Ustaŝe, the local Croatian fascists, in November 1942. Nemon seldom spoke about the loss of his family, although the musician and composer Ronald Senator [1926–2015], a close friend, recalled that he was

> profoundly affected, even if he sometimes concealed his pain with a mask, saying with a cynical smile and a backward tilt of his fine head how miniscule was Planet Earth in the infinite vastness of the cosmos and how much fuss we made about it. [Young & Hale, 2018, p. 135]

Nemon's sense of loss and the burden of having survived dominated the art he made after the war. Senator surmised that "with the guilt of the survivor, Oscar recoiled from creating experimental works of personal feeling" (Young & Hale, 2018, p. 135), and, instead, he concentrated on exploring and memorialising the human figure through portraiture, sculpting an astonishing number of eminent figures from the British establishment. Despite this successful career and his long-standing association with Winston Churchill and the British Royal Family, Nemon always remained something of an outsider; by character not a man who found joining in easy, he was never fully accepted by the British art world (Sebba, 2011).

But this was all in the future. Invited to meet Melanie Klein, Nemon must have been both excited and intrigued by the opportunity to sculpt another leading member of the psychoanalytic community. Klein, now 57 years old, was at the height of her powers and a leading figure in the British Psychoanalytical Society. The year 1932 had seen the publication of her book *The Psycho-Analysis of Children,* an event that Ernest Jones, when writing to congratulate her, referred to as "a momentous event in the history of psycho-analysis and particularly in the achievement of our Society among which we are proud to count you as an honoured member" (Grosskurth, 1985, p. 194). Paula Heimann [1899–1982], later a leading psychoanalyst and supporter of Klein, recalled that during meetings of the British Society "Melanie Klein, Joan Riviere and Susan Isaacs used to sit in the front row, and it was obvious that Melanie Klein was at that time very highly regarded by most people" (King, 1989, p. 3).

But despite this comfortable eminence, Klein continued to be haunted by personal tragedy and was beset with professional difficulties.

Virginia Woolf, a perceptive observer of humanity, had met Klein for the first time in March the same year at the celebrations for the 25th anniversary of the British Society in the Savoy Hotel. A few days later she invited Klein to dinner and subsequently wrote in her diary that she was

> a woman of character and force and some submerged—how shall I say—not craft, but subtlety: something working underground. A pull, a twist, like an undertow: menacing. A bluff grey haired lady, with large bright imaginative eyes. [Bell, 1984, p. 209]

In this curious characterisation, Woolf does not allude directly to Klein's depression, but Klein's friends all agreed that, in spite of the birth of her first grandson Michael in 1937, she had again been deeply depressed over the previous few years, recalling the intense melancholy of her early married life.

The first half of the 1930s had been a time of loss. In May 1933, Sándor Ferenczi, Klein's first analyst, died in Budapest. In the same year Kloetzel, Klein's former lover from Berlin days, emigrated to Palestine; Klein was never to see him again. The following year, 1934, Klein's oldest son, Hans, who had always reminded her of Emanuel, was killed in a tragic accident while walking in the Tatra Mountains (Grosskurth, 1985, p. 215). Klein was so overwhelmed by grief that she felt unable to leave London for the funeral, and, according to Eric, Klein's surviving son, Hans's death remained a source of grief to his mother for the rest of her life. In a touching regression, she confided her most painful feelings to Paula Heimann, a relative stranger at the time, rather than to one of her English friends, because, she told Heimann, "the English were too alien, and anyhow they could not speak German" (King, 1989, p. 3). She showed Heimann her most treasured possessions, Emanuel's poems (Grosskurth, 1985, p. 380), a concrete link between the deaths of her brother and her son.

For Klein, each episode of depression revived the sorrows and griefs from the past, in particular the deaths of her sister Sidonie and her brother Emanuel. Although Klein's friends and colleagues insist on her gaiety and vivacity, and, in the words of Adrian Stokes, "despite [her] lonely and intellectual power [she] was pre-eminent in her enjoyment of people, in her looks, in her responsiveness" (Stokes, 1960), melancholy was integral to her personality and the key to her creativity. In the second half of the 1930s, following her son's tragic death, Klein wrote some of her most influential papers, including "A Contribution to the Psychogenesis of Manic-Depressive States" (1935), "Weaning" (1936), "Love, Guilt and Reparation" (1937) and "Mourning and Its Relation to Manic-Depressive States" (1940), all of which emerged out of her own deep personal suffering (Grosskurth, 1985, p. 231). These "triumphs in adversity" were hard won and perhaps go some way to explain why Klein fought so tenaciously to ensure that her ideas and her work were fully accepted by the psychoanalytic establishment.

In 1939, Klein's fight for professional recognition and anxiety about the security of her legacy were very real concerns. Antipathy towards Klein in the psychoanalytic communities of Vienna and Berlin was of long standing, and now in London she began to come under attack as well. Melitta, Klein's daughter, had qualified with distinction as a doctor in Berlin in 1927 and joined her mother in London the next year, followed after some delay by her husband, Walter Schmideberg. Initially the relationship between the three was amicable, but after Melitta began to train as a psychoanalyst herself, the situation gradually deteriorated. Melitta and Edward Glover, a powerful figure in the British Society and Melitta's analyst, became increasingly antagonistic towards Klein, ultimately resulting in a permanent estrangement between mother and daughter. The bitter feelings that Melitta felt towards her mother, which she expressed so publicly, must have been a source of great pain and sorrow to Klein, but, despite this painful antipathy between mother and daughter, Melanie kept a photograph of Melitta as a young girl beside her bed until her death (Grosskurth, 1985, p. 411). However, it was not just familial rivalry; the difficult situation was greatly compounded by the arrival in London of the European analysts fleeing persecution, who were uniformly hostile to Klein's ideas. Beginning after the Reichstag fire in 1933, the exodus from Europe continued throughout the 1930s, culminating in the arrival of Anna and Sigmund Freud on 6 June 1938, by which time fully one third of the analysts in the British Psychoanalytical Society were from central Europe. The atmosphere in the Society became progressively more fractious. Although Klein played her part in sponsoring and supporting the European analysts, she was in no doubt about the difficulties this would create for her. The London Institute of Psychoanalysis, she is reported to have said in conversation with Clare Winnicott, "will never be the same again, this is a disaster" (Grosskurth, 1985, p. 241).

What was Oscar Nemon—an impoverished refugee preoccupied with the dire situation in Europe, fearful for the fate of his family in Croatia and concerned for his own security in the United Kingdom, under threat from his future wife's hostile anti-Semitic parents (Young & Hale, 2018, p. 103)—to make of this powerful, troubled woman? We do not know who introduced the sculptor and the analyst, but it may perhaps have been Ernest Jones [1878–1958], then the President of the British Psychoanalytical Society and a close colleague of Klein's. Nemon had known Ernest Jones since 1935 and had made a sculpture of him; Nemon also met his wife-to-be, Patricia Villiers-Stuart, who was a patient of Jones, at a party in the analyst's house sometime in late 1936. We do not know why Klein agreed to go ahead with the sculpture, although apparently Nemon needed all his famous charm to persuade a reluctant Klein to proceed. Nor do we know how much of Klein's fraught professional situation and personal history Nemon understood. It is possible Klein felt bulldozed into agreeing against her better judgement, flattered perhaps by the knowledge that Nemon had previously sculpted both Freud and her first analyst Sándor Ferenczi. There are hints that the relationship between the two was strained from the start. Nemon was later to recall, when Phyllis Grosskurth interviewed him by telephone on a visit to London in 1980 (McMullan, personal communication, 2011), that

> Melanie had a noticeable tendency to pomposity and was easily capable of self-righteous behaviour. Perhaps these qualities were manifest in my work and caused her some discomfort. [Grosskurth, 1985, p. 200]

It was Nemon's practice to work initially from life. He would begin by talking to his subject, asking questions and telling stories, "all the time shaping the little oval of clay—small enough to lie in the palm of his hand, or be held up on a stick, which became the first sketch" (Nemon, 2019). The next step was a clay head, often life-size or larger, which he would create and modify in the studio using sketches and other material as a guide; if things went well, the clay head would be cast in plaster and, finally, in bronze. He was a perfectionist, obsessively moulding the clay in his hands, often barely able to finish a piece and put it aside (Young & Hale, 2018, p. 82). In the case of the Klein head, Nemon also had a tantalisingly brief, silent cine film to aid his memory, perhaps taken by Jessie Stonor, Nemon's girlfriend at the time, who is known to have owned a cine camera (Young, 2017a). The film, which is now owned by the Melanie Klein Trust (Klein, 1939), perfectly demonstrates Nemon's technique with his sitter. Klein and Nemon are shown walking and conversing in the garden of Klein's house in Clifton Hill; Klein is captured certainly looking more careworn, awkward, and self-conscious, always aware of the watching camera, but smiling, laughing, and talking, posing in profile and full face, so that her features are variously lit by the spring sunshine. The impression given is of Nemon being polite, convivial, and gracious but Klein not really enjoying the experience even at this early stage. Later photographs, perhaps also taken by Jessie Stonor, show Nemon working on the clay model in the garden (Figure 31) and Nemon and Klein standing on either side of the plaster bust (Figure 32).

The twice life-size head appears to be a good likeness, inclined slightly to one side and poised delicately on the finger and thumb of one hand, capturing perhaps a characteristic gesture of Klein's hinted at in the photograph itself. But Klein apparently showed great alarm when confronted with the bust and is said to have "loathed the head, which she hid in the attic for some years before destroying it" (Grosskurth, 1985, p. 200). This account of Klein's reaction, given in Grosskurth's biography, is unreferenced: Eric Klein, Melanie's surviving son, is said to have provided Grosskurth with many details of Klein's personal life during her research and may be the source of this information (Brimblecombe, personal communication, 2011), although the truth of the account is now impossible to verify and, inevitably, it raises more questions than it answers. How exactly did a 57-year-old woman manhandle a heavy plaster bust into the attic? Was she helped, and if so, by whom? How did she destroy the bust, an act requiring considerable physical force? And, finally, "loathe" is a powerful word—why did Klein hate the bust so much?

Nemon believed that the vocations of the portrait sculptor and of the psychoanalyst were closely allied (Nemon, 2019). In his portraits of analysts he sought, he said, to create studies that were informed by

Figure 31   Oscar Nemon, aged 33 (1939). *Unknown photographer; possibly Jessie Stonor. [Copyright Oscar Nemon Estate, with the kind permission of Aurelia Young.]*

but travelled beyond the individual's published works and public persona, challenging the viewer to see the sitter in a new light. Melanie Klein's granddaughter, Diana Brimblecombe, cannot understand what her grandmother disliked about the sculpture: "It seems a very good likeness and not unkind in any way", although she added, "I remember, she was quite a vain person" (Brimblecombe, personal communication, 2011). Perhaps Nemon was correct in his supposition that some of the self-righteousness he detected in Klein's character was apparent in the bust, or possibly he managed to capture something of Klein's personal and professional difficulties that she did not like being made so explicit. However, one incontrovertible feature of the bust is that it was large, and perhaps it was the very fact of its size that was at the root of Klein's dislike of it. It was Nemon's custom to make the plaster model either life-size or twice life-size, and he may have chosen to make the larger version in response to Klein's appearance itself: she is often described as having a large face and large features. But, in reality, Klein was a petite woman, whose innovative work was based upon her empathy for and sensitivity to the emotional lives of small children. In the photograph (Figure 32) she does indeed appear to be dwarfed by what may have seemed to her to be a monstrous white head. Furthermore, in sculpture, size is often associated with hubris, an inflated sense of worth, a boastful and exaggerated self-esteem. Although Klein was forceful in the promotion and defence of her theories and ideas, she was too sensitive and too in tune with her own imperfections as a woman and mother to be susceptible to these deceptions and may actively have resented a representation of herself that in any way suggested this. Perhaps here we have an explanation for Klein's loathing, which otherwise seems so inexplicable.

It is of interest that Klein was not alone among Nemon's psychoanalytic subjects in being dissatisfied with the sculptor's efforts: both René Laforgue [1894–1962], one of the founders of the Paris Psychoanalytical Society, and Paul Federn were bemused by their respective busts. Many years after Nemon created his bust, Laforgue wrote:

> It is funny to see a sculptor take possession of your head, making it look naively in the air, slightly inspired. And then having to pretend that his

head belongs to you. I don't recognise myself in this masterpiece. Yet Nemon made the best portrait of Freud as well as the one of Churchill. Maybe I am not connected to myself? Who knows . . . [Young & Hale, 2018, p. 90]

Paul Federn was more forthright, offering a rather brutal critique of his sculpture and complaining to Nemon that:

The head was exquisite three weeks before you finished it, then your spirit of wanting to be more than true, mixed with some self-destruction, spitefulness and arrogance got into you. You have made the bust into something ridiculous, cheery and wise but on the whole into the unpleasant head of a Jew. [Young & Hale, 2018, p. 69]

There follows a detailed list of the faults that Federn perceived in the bust, including his tilted head, a consequence of one-sided hearing loss,

Figure 32 Oscar Nemon and Melanie Klein, London (1939). *Unknown photographer; possibly Jessie Stonor.* [*Copyright Oscar Nemon Estate, with the kind permission of Aurelia Young.*]

and his wooden, silent mouth (Young & Hale, 2018, p. 69), both features, interestingly, related to his main tasks as a psychoanalyst—listening and speaking. Whatever their criticisms, however, the two analysts saw value in Nemon's work, and neither of them went to the extreme of destroying the representations of themselves.

And that may have been the end of the story, except that, in 2016, two badly damaged low-relief sculptures of Melanie Klein in profile were found, wrapped together in newspaper, in the bottom drawer of a filing cabinet among the possessions of Hanna Segal after her death. They were subsequently given by the Segal family to the Melanie Klein Trust (Melanie Klein Trust, personal communication, 2016). Returned to the light of day after being hidden from view for nearly 80 years, these bas-relief sculptures are austere and classical in their simplicity (Figure 33). The portraits are unsigned but have been positively identified as the work of Oscar Nemon by Daniel Zec, an expert on his work, and by Alice Nemon-Stuart, Nemon's daughter-in-law (Young, personal communication, 2017b). There is little information about their provenance. Presumably, they were made by Nemon in 1939, at the same time as he was working on the more conventional bust of Klein, and came into the possession of Hanna Segal, the chair of the

Figure 33 Low-relief sculptures of Melanie Klein, aged 57 (1939). *Sculptor Oscar Nemon; restored by Jim Kempton, 2018; photograph taken by Sarah Lane.* [*Copyright Melanie Klein Trust, reprinted with permission.*]

Figure 34 Oscar Nemon and Domenico Borghese (1924). *Unknown photographer.*
[*Copyright the Oscar Nemon Estate, reprinted with the kind permission of Aurelia Young.*]

Melanie Klein Trust and a lifelong friend and advocate of Klein's ideas, after Klein's death in 1960. Klein's papers were deposited by Hanna Segal in the Wellcome Library in 1984, but, for unknown reasons, she retained the sculptures, never making the fact of their existence public. The reliefs are the only sculpted portraits of Klein made during her lifetime to have survived. Nemon produced medallions and low-relief sculptures throughout his working life and clearly enjoyed working in this form. Aged 18 he was photographed making an extraordinarily accomplished low-relief sculpture of the famous Italian baritone Domenico Borghese (Figure 34); this is presumably the reason why he created these sculptures of Klein, since there is nothing to lead us to believe that Klein specifically commissioned them. Why she decided to keep them, although she evidently did not preserve them with any great care or love, considering their state when they were found, is yet another mystery.

* * *

B, Sacksel.

Figure 35   Melanie Klein, aged 62 (1944). *Bertl Sachsel, London. [Copyright Melanie Klein Trust, reprinted with permission.]*

The personalised attacks on Klein by the European analysts reached a venomous pitch in the spring of 1942, culminating in the "Controversial Discussions". These were a protracted series of meetings in London, often characterised by vehement argument, between the Viennese school and the supporters of Melanie Klein. Although they failed to reach any theoretical agreement, a political settlement was established that persists in the British Psychoanalytical Society to this day. In the year these formal meetings concluded, 1944, the photographer Bertl Sachsel [1901–1989] captured two remarkable images of Klein (Figures 35 & 36). Despite years of unremitting aggressive personal attacks, the

Figure 36 Melanie Klein, aged 62 (1944). *Bertl Sachsel, London.* [*Copyright Melanie Klein Trust, reprinted with permission.*]

images show nothing of this: Klein's face is soft and gentle, the expression tranquil and reflective, the gaze far away, with just a hint of a smile. The face is lit by natural light, and the portraits are a study in mid-tones, soft greys and shades of white; unlike the earlier Lambert portrait, the contrast levels are lowered, subduing the mood and giving Klein a more introspective quality.

Born in Vienna, Bertl Sachsel spent her youth in Berlin but fled persecution, arriving in England in the late 1930s and marrying an Englishman, Felix Gaye, an engineer with Rolls Royce (Gaye, 2019). Many of her relatives were later killed in the Holocaust. Her only child, a son,

Adrian, was born in 1944, a year after her marriage and the same year as she took the images of Klein, which were among her earliest portrait photographs. The couple later separated, and Sachsel spent the rest of her life in Cambridge, alone apart from visits by Adrian in the school holidays. Her devotion to photography had been triggered when she was a young woman at art school in Vienna, suddenly captivated by the shadow of a cup on a Chinese map. She used natural light exclusively, which gives her photographs their characteristic soft, natural quality, and she only ever used a standard Rolleiflex camera. In ways reminiscent of Aladár Székely, Sachsel was also interested in hands and what they conveyed in terms of character and meaning, famously making several photographic studies of Yehudi Menuhin's hands.

Jeanne Wakatsuki [b. 1934], a Japanese–American novelist whose husband was in the American Air Force and was stationed near Cambridge in the late 1950s, recalls Sachsel as a tiny, shy woman who spoke in heavily accented English, with smiling, mischievous eyes, quick and sprightly on her feet despite a stooped back and a limp (Wakatsuki, 2019). The two women spent many evenings together listening to Mozart and Schubert, and Wakatsuki remembers Sachsel's warmth, understanding, and forgiveness. She recalls two German-language students who stayed with the photographer one summer; when they discovered at breakfast one morning that Sachsel was Jewish, they were overcome with anguish and remorse. Sachsel comforted them. '"Why do you cry?' she said gently. 'It is not your crime. But you must go home and tell your parents you have spent your summer with a Jew, a Jew who didn't spit at you and treated you well. Then, they can cry, not you'" (Wakatsuki, 2019). Despite knowing many famous nuclear physicists in pre-war Berlin, Max Planck and Robert Oppenheimer among them, Sachsel was a convinced, lifelong pacifist, ardently opposed to nuclear armaments, and she told the two students to honour her by fighting against nuclear weapons; one of them, at least, became active in the German anti-nuclear weapons campaign.

In an interview for the *Cambridge Daily News* on the 16th of November 1960, in words reminiscent of Oscar Nemon, Sachsel spoke about her approach to photographing her subjects:

Her one aim is to make people look natural. . . . She feels that people are less self-conscious in their own homes and the setting gives an indication of their character which [she] finds useful in deciding on the right way to take the photographs. "Each person has hundreds of expressions and I am concerned with getting the one which is most characteristic." . . . She likes, for this reason, to talk to her subjects for a time before attempting to photograph them. [Gaye, 2019]

In the same interview, Sachsel confessed that although she spends a large part of her time photographing other people, she has no photograph of herself, because "she dislikes facing the camera".

* * *

Sometime in the late 1940s, shortly after Bertl Sachsel had taken these photographs, Klein was painted by the Hungarian-born artist Olga Székely-Kovács, better known under her married name, Olga Dormandi [1900–1971]. Despite Klein's difficult personal and professional circumstances and the desperate state of the wider world, the three series of portraits from the 1940s—the low reliefs by Oscar Nemon, the photographs by Bertl Sachsel, and the painting by Olga Dormandi—all share a remarkably similar atmosphere, untroubled, calm, even serene.

Olga Dormandi grew up in a home in Budapest frequented by artists, musicians, and poets, which was also the centre of the Hungarian Psychoanalytical Society. She was deeply immersed in the psychoanalytic world: her mother, Vilma, was analysed by Sándor Ferenczi, who later became a popular family friend, and subsequently trained as an analyst herself; her sister Alice, also a psychoanalyst, was the leading expert on children's mental health in Hungary between the wars and married Michael Balint, another psychoanalyst; and Olga's daughter, Judith Dupont, was later to become a psychoanalyst living and working in Paris (Dormandi, 2019). Olga had a difficult childhood: her mother, Vilma [1883–1940], had been married against her will, aged 15, to a cousin twenty-two years her senior, and her three children, Alice, Olga, and Ferencz, were born over the next four years. Worn out by the repeated pregnancies, Vilma became ill with tuberculosis and was admitted to a sanatorium, where she met her second husband, Frederic Kovács. After

Figure 37 Olga Dormandi (*c.*1948). *Self-portrait.* [*Copyright Olga Dormandi Estate, reprinted with kind permission of Pierre Dupont.*]

a difficult divorce and remarriage, she lost custody of her children, including Olga, who was only about 5 years old at the time. Badly treated and separated from their mother for several years, the children were reunited with her only sometime around 1910 and were subsequently adopted by their stepfather. Like Oscar Nemon's, Olga's talent for painting was apparent early in her life, and after art school she trained with Róbert Berény. Her self-portrait (Figure 37) was painted at much the same time as she painted Klein and shows her holding the tools of her trade; portrayed as sharp and thoughtful, there is a clear sense of scepticism, and the mood is unsettling, questioning.

The collapse of the Austro-Hungarian Empire at the end of the First World War was followed by political upheaval in Hungary, which made life very difficult for the Hungarian analysts and had been one factor in Klein's decision to leave Budapest for Berlin in 1921. But it was the rise of National Socialism that was to result in the total destruction of this cultured and civilised world. In 1924, Olga married Ladislas Dormandi, a publisher, translator, and author, and the couple, with their only daughter Judith, remained in Budapest until 1938, when they eventually fled to Paris, managing to survive the war there. Alice and Michael Balint escaped to Manchester, where Alice died tragically a few months later. Vilma travelled to Paris as well at the invitation of Princess Marie Bonaparte, but, a broken woman, returned to Budapest, where she died shortly after, in 1940.

In 1923, as a young woman, Dormandi had painted Sándor Ferenczi, by now an intimate of the family and well known to all the children, who was the leader of the Hungarian Psychoanalytical Society and also the analyst with whom Klein had first started treatment. Some time later in 1931, Oscar Nemon was to sculpt a bust of Ferenczi. Both the painting and bust are now lost, presumed to have been destroyed during the liberation of Budapest by the Red Army in the winter of 1944–45, but they survive in an extraordinary photograph (Figure 38) showing Ferenczi and Nemon standing on either side of Nemon's newly completed bust and below the Dormandi portrait, which hangs, partially obscured, on the wall behind them, above a china display cabinet. Although Ferenczi's house still stands near the centre of Buda and now accommodates the International Ferenczi Center, during the liberation of the city the area around the house saw particularly heavy fighting. Ilona Félszeghy [1892–1988], a Hungarian psychoanalyst, was the last person to see the portrait of Ferenczi. Shortly after the liberation of the city, she crossed the near-frozen Danube from Pest to Buda via a Soviet-controlled pontoon bridge to discover Ferenczi's house in ruins, with only the staircase and one wall remaining standing and with papers and manuscripts scattered in the rubble. The portrait of Ferenczi still hung on the surviving wall. She retrieved the papers, intending to return the following day for the portrait, but when she did, the portrait

Figure 38 Oscar Nemon and Sándor Ferenczi (1931). *Unknown photographer.*
[*Copyright Oscar Nemon Estate, reprinted with kind permission of Aurelia Young.*]

had vanished (Dupont, 2013, p. 2). Félszeghy (Félszeghy, 2019) looked after the papers for the next few years, giving them to Michael Balint when he first returned to Budapest after the war, in 1948; they were subsequently translated by Judith Dupont, Olga's daughter, and are now preserved as the Ferenczi Archive in the Freud Museum in London (Freud Museum, 2018).

In the same way as Oscar Nemon's friendship with Freud gave him access to many other psychoanalytic subjects, Olga Dormandi's family associations meant that, as well as Ferenczi and Klein, she painted several other psychoanalysts, including her brother-in-law Michael Balint, Marie Bonaparte, Marion Milner, and Elizabeth Severn. We do not know who commissioned the portrait of Klein or how artist and psychoanalyst first met. It is possible that Klein may have been acquainted with Olga Dormandi during the time she lived in Budapest (1910 to 1921), though for most of this decade Olga was a teenager, and by the time Klein left Budapest, Olga was only just starting out on her career as an artist.

Dormandi's portrait of Klein (Figure 39) is now owned by Melanie Klein's granddaughters, who talk with affection about the portrait;

Figure 39   Melanie Klein, aged 66 (c.1948). *Olga Dormandi, London. [Reprinted with kind permission of Diana Brimblecombe and Hazel Bentall.]*

this, they say, is how they remember their granny: "auntish-like, granny-like, she looks homely, and that large comforting bosom that she had" (Brimblecombe & Bentall, 2014). Unusually for a portrait artist, Dormandi would work from memory. An American journalist who interviewed Dormandi in 1965 wrote:

> Having taken mental notes of the movements, expressions, the relaxation and tension of the body she draws from memory the build-up of the face, working alone without the model. [Joffee Goodfriend, 1965, p. 35]

In not working from life, perhaps something is lost, and this portrait of Klein is certainly non-confrontational, or, in the words of the art critic and ex-patient of Klein, Adrian Stokes, "it makes no statement" (Sayers, 2012, p. 120). The painting is impressionistic, suffused with autumnal sunlight, the background glowing with rich, warm colour. Klein sits very upright, recalling the description of Nellie Wollfheim, with an enigmatic smile, a string of pearls around her neck, and holding a small, leather-bound book. She looks directly at the artist and at us with a quizzical, half-knowing expression. The way in which the painting is lit is unusual: sunshine pours through the window immediately behind Klein, dazzling us, so to speak, blurring the outlines of the face and hair, so that Klein's features are difficult to make out clearly. There is no overt trace of grief or melancholy, and, perhaps for this reason, it was an image that Klein cherished and preserved. Olga Dormandi did not confront her subjects with uncomfortable truths. In a restatement of that fundamental tension inherent in the relationship between artist and subject, the conflict between the vision and integrity of the artist and the wishes of the subject, how he or she wants to be commemorated, Dormandi said, in the same interview, that

> If he [the artist] only creates something for himself, then he's not an artist! He must communicate with people. There must be a coming together of an inner and outer reality in balance. [Joffee Goodfriend, 1965, p. 35]

However, there is a subtlety to this painting, which is easily overlooked. First, there is the ambiguity in the face, a consequence of the novel way in which the painting is lit; second, the colouring of the painting is also curious, in some ways not unlike the colour choices in Dormandi's own self-portrait. The warm reds and browns are in stark contrast to the mass of cold, almost icy blue of Klein's blouse; these are colours that are polar opposites, from different ends of the colour spectrum. Perhaps in using light and colour, rather than line and form, Dormandi was trying to convey something of her sense of Klein in a way calculated not to antagonise her subject: complexity and ambivalence or, recalling Virginia Woolf's comments, something hidden, concealed beneath the superficial warmth? Whatever the explanation, the balance struck by Dormandi was a successful one—much more successful, as we shall see, than the only other painter to portray Klein, William Coldstream.

CHAPTER SIX

Later life

London, 1951 to 1960

The year 1952 was an important one for Klein—the year of her 70th birthday, a time for taking stock and planning for the future. A celebratory dinner organised by Ernest Jones was held at Kettner's restaurant, in Soho, in late March, and a book, *Developments in Psycho-Analysis,* as well as a Special Issue of the *International Journal of Psychoanalysis,* followed later in the year. But behind the celebratory atmosphere Klein remained "fearful for the future of her ideas, and concentrated increasingly on building up around her a nucleus of gifted and devoted followers" (Grosskurth, 1985, p. 408). This was also a year for commemoration: the *Sunday Times* asked the portrait photographer Douglas Glass to photograph Klein for the *Portrait Gallery* series in the Sunday supplement, and Adrian Stokes commissioned the English realist artist William Coldstream to paint a portrait of his analyst.

Douglas Glass [1901–1978] was a bohemian New Zealander, born in Auckland but of Scottish ancestry. After varied work as a cowhand, sheep shearer, drover, and salesman, he came to England in 1926 and trained at the Central School of Art. In the early months after the end of the Second World War, he was the official photographer for the UN

Relief and Rehabilitation Administration in Germany, documenting the reality of life for displaced persons in post-war Europe. However, disillusioned with bureaucratic inhumanity, he left the following year, with his young family, for the Australian outback. In 1949 some early portrait photographs he had taken came to the attention of the editor of the *Sunday Times*, who persuaded Glass to come back to London, and for the next twelve years he photographed a host of eminent people for the newspaper. This corpus of work was to make his name, and his first exhibition, in 1953, a year after his photographs of Klein were taken, drew an audience of 10,000, some likening his work documenting the New Elizabethan Age to that of Holbein's commemoration of the Tudor court (Mellor, 1978, p. 13). By his own admission, Glass was "extremely loquacious, [with] a certain colonial attitude to the Queen's English, which sometimes caused discomfort to the more delicate of his English friends" (Mellor, 1978, p. 4). He thought of himself as a "sentimental socialist [and] believed that man could get a better deal" (Mellor, 1978, p. 7). He was, he said, "not interested in photography as such; [but was] more interested in the subject, if photography gets in the way of revealing the sitter I am disappointed" (Mellor, 1978, p. 5).

His self-portrait (Figure 40) is carefully composed; he sits assertively, bucolic yet sophisticated, surrounded by a collection of carefully chosen books, many of them volumes of poetry, his own photograph of the composer Ralph Vaughan Williams, reproductions of works by Picasso and Miró, and, by his right elbow, an incongruous imperial lion, perhaps there in recognition of his colonial origins. The greater-than-life–sized, grimacing Devon fisherman he has chosen to share his portrait with was one of the first images to bring him to public attention, part of the series entitled "Drake's Descendants" commissioned by Lord Clark of the War Artists Advisory Committee in the dark days of 1940 and intended to emphasise the heroism of the ascendant common man.

The images of Melanie Klein taken by Douglas Glass (Figures 41 to 43) are the first of the three sets of justly famous iconic photographs taken of her in old age. His portraits, for the first time since Klein's childhood, capture something of the gaiety and liveliness alluded to by

Figure 40   Douglas Glass (late 1950s). *Self-portrait.* [*Copyright J C C Glass, reprinted with permission.*]

her friends and colleagues. The portraits are characterised by intense contrast, dramatic shadow, and what can sometimes feel like a slightly contrived range of mood. In the background is a bookcase, a reference that occurs repeatedly in these later portraits. Klein has taken great care with her appearance; she is elegant, wearing discreet jewellery, and her hair is beautifully groomed. In the first image (Figure 41), the mood is playful, the expression of the face open, calling to mind the 8-year-old Melanie with a lapful of flowers. She sits informally, with chin on hand, in an echo of the pose chosen both by Oscar Nemon and by Bertl Sachsel. The second image (Figure 42) is wistful

Figure 41 Melanie Klein, aged 70 (1952). *Douglas Glass, London.* [*Copyright Melanie Klein Trust, reprinted with permission.*]

rather than sad but reprises the by now familiar reflective face with an averted, distant gaze. The third and final image (Figure 43) is the most unusual and the most disturbing. Klein's brow is furrowed: one could imagine that Glass has asked her to feign anger, or possibly he has just been indiscreet. But there is also something very real in this picture and in the expression, something particularly haunting in the eyes. Of all the images of Klein, this one is unique in the painful intensity of the gaze. Revealingly perhaps, Klein kept only a proof copy of this image and did not request a formal portrait photograph, as she did for the first two images.

Figure 42   Melanie Klein, aged 70 (1952). *Douglas Glass, London.* [*Copyright Melanie Klein Trust, reprinted with permission.*]

* * *

The other artistic venture of 1952 was the second major attempt by a significant artist of the day to portray Klein. Sir William Coldstream [1908–1987] was a distinguished realist painter and arts teacher who had a major influence on the development of the arts in England during the twentieth century (Laughton, 2004). Born in Northumberland, the youngest child of a country doctor, Coldstream grew up in north London and, having been refused admission to university to study medicine, trained at the Slade (Figure 44). In 1937 he co-founded the short-lived,

Figure 43 Melanie Klein, aged 70 (1952). *Douglas Glass, London.* [*Copyright Melanie Klein Trust, reprinted with permission.*]

but influential, Euston Road School, and during the war he served on the War Artists Advisory Committee. In 1949 he was appointed Principal and Professor of Fine Art at the Slade, remaining there for the rest of his working life, although also holding positions as Vice-Chair of the Arts Council, Trustee of the National Gallery, and Chair of the British Film Institute. The "Coldstream Reports", produced during the many years he was chair of the National Advisory Council on Arts Education, were responsible for fundamental, wide-ranging reforms in arts education. An establishment figure if ever there was one, he was, in the words of his friends, deeply serious although not solemn, uncommonly intel-

Figure 44   William Coldstream (1956). *Walter Stoneman, London. [Copyright National Portrait Gallery, London, reprinted with permission.]*

ligent but with "a sense of the ridiculous and an impish perception of the everyday incongruities of life" (Gowring, 1987, p. 29). In the words of William Townsend, a lifelong friend:

> Beneath all the badinage and jocular cynicism, and not very far beneath, Bill is one of the kindest men, full of understanding and sympathy and helpfulness. And I understand so well the substructure of the puritan tradition, the austerity of attitude that controls an easy sensuousness; the intellectual integrity that is all sinew that I think will maintain him in his standards and purposes when many others will have slipped off into easier and showier successes. [Laughton, 2004, p. ix]

From his earliest years as a student at the Slade, Coldstream had been interested in real appearances—an outlook completely out of step with contemporary trends. In Coldstream's own words:

> Painters had been taught to regard all artistic movements, except those away from realism, as artistically reactionary. A direct realistic approach was to be considered to be something which had been finished with at the end of the nineteenth century. [Coldstream, 1938, p. 102]

In the mid-1930s he decided he would, in future, only paint "living subjects from life and paint them straight" (Gowring, 1962, p. 7). This personal credo, honest and clear-sighted, was supported by a very particular technique: thick pigment, high colour, and the cursive line were all abandoned in favour of a small palette of simple pigments applied in straight, parallel brush strokes. He was meticulous about putting the right thing in the right place, measuring and marking out the canvas, allowing the exact shape and position of different components of a composition to be related precisely one to another, and it was with this "regular and impartial net that he caught the visual facts" (Gowring, 1962, p. 15). Despite such exactitude and extreme deliberation, his work was "not academic or mechanical" (Lampert, 1984, p. 2); on the contrary, fellow artist Euan Uglow would praise the beauty and poetry of his painting (Uglow, 1987, p. 27). These slow and painstaking methods meant that individual paintings might take many months to complete, and it was Coldstream's practice to work within "the discipline of fixed times for his sittings". "I feel", he said, "that the actual passage of time in some way or other is necessary in a painting" (Lampert, 1984, p. 5).

When it came to portraiture, Coldstream's view was that the essential characteristics of a good portraitist were "a passionate interest in building up the work from the particular". The power of a portrait, he thought, "was not due to distortion in any ordinary sense of the word but in the extraordinary fact that a touch laid on with conviction transmits this conviction, with all its imaginary reserves, to the spectator" (Laughton, 2004, pp. 140, 142). In the words of Adrian Stokes, a close friend, the subject of a Coldstream portrait

> is not to be interpreted, explained or flattered . . . she develops undistorted into a personage neither idealized nor debased . . . the rejec-

tion or twisting of basic appearances was inconceivable. [Stokes, 1962, p. 15]

Graham Bell, friend, fellow artist, and co-founder of the Euston Road School with Coldstream, summed up the artist's approach:

Coldstream's strength is not in the bold black line or in gobbets of paint nor in caricature-like exaggerations, but in the logical way he works. His greatest asset is the faith he has in his imaginative power to recreate the personalities of his sitters. His effects are achieved almost in spite of himself. His is the art that conceals art. . . . He concentrates on the visible characteristics of his subjects. That he achieves an uncanny insight into his sitters is a tribute to the power of his imagination to make the most of the finest variations of emphasis. [Bell, 1939, p. 24]

Adrian Stokes [1902–1972], friend, pupil, and long-standing admirer and advocate of Coldstream's art, was a writer, art critic, and painter who straddled the ground between psychoanalysis and modernism (Sayers, 2015b). He was a patient of Melanie Klein from December 1929 until 1935, and briefly again in 1946, and he remained in regular contact with his analyst throughout the rest of her life, incorporating many of her ideas into his art criticism, indebted to her for facilitating the publication of his work and also for arranging the treatment of his disturbed daughter, Ariadne. Stokes was known for his radical "carving aesthetic", in which he understood the best of Renaissance architecture and sculpture to be an attempt to bring to life the physical material, the stone, out of which a building or sculpture is made, the artist's moulding and carving of the material freeing it, allowing it to flower, "to bear infants, to give the fruit of the land and sea" (Stokes, 1932, p. 40). Later in his life, he used Klein's concept of part-objects as a way of thinking about painting and architecture. In a famous passage, he likened the way we internalise the experience of others as loved or hated part-objects to a coral reef:

Ceaseless seas of experience construct the coral mind . . . we are made up by these minute and accumulated deposits no more than by those monster forms, beneficent and murderous which we in fantasy have swallowed, incorporated so that they lie together inside, sometimes separate, sometimes in union, to whose needs, to whose natures, all subsequent experience is referred. [Sayers, 2015b, p. 175]

He came to understand that, after the initial attack on the physical material of their art—the stone or canvas—the artist's job is to bring together these disparate elements, to forge them into a whole (Sayers, 2015a, p. 1022), leading "us to experience from art a feeling of oneness with the world" (Stokes, 1955, p. 37).

Adrian Stokes would in time come to consider Coldstream to be "a great modern master" (Stokes, 1962, p. 16), and, on the occasion of Klein's 70th birthday, he commissioned Coldstream to paint a portrait of his analyst, as a very public way of honouring her. Klein was touched by Stokes's suggestion, and in January 1952 she wrote to him:

> Thank you very much for your [portrait] offer,—I very much appreciate it. I have given some thought to it and discussed it with a few friends who agree with your arguments in favour of this suggestion. Although I am reluctant to accept the financial demand it imposes on you and my other friends I am inclined to accept because I hope that the money might be collected from subscriptions. My friend Mrs. Riviere is very interested in this plan and would like to discuss it with you. She is going to get in touch with you directly—probably in a week or two. In the meantime again many thanks for your offer and the very kind thoughts which it implies. [Sayers, 2012, p. 119]

Joan Riviere [1883–1962], who Klein asked to liaise with Stokes, was another important influence during the gestation of the portrait. She was a prominent psychoanalyst, a translator of Freud, and an articulate exponent of Klein's ideas (Hughes, 1991, p. 1). Feared by some for her sharp tongue and the severity of her judgements (Hughes, 1991, p. 33), she was cultured and discerning (Hughes, 1991, p. 6), with a personal talent for drawing and design (Hughes, 1991, p. 5). At the suggestion of Adrian Stokes, she went to see two paintings by Coldstream, *Man with a Beard* (Figure 45) and *Havildar Ajmer Singh* (Figure 46), now both in the Tate Collection. She subsequently wrote to Stokes in February 1952 about her reaction to the paintings. "I admired them extremely as pictures; I thought they were exquisite as you said, so rare in that they had not a trace of vulgarity—a quality which seemed unique among all the surrounding works!" But, as she explained to Stokes, she feared that

Figure 45 *Man with a Beard* (1939). *William Coldstream.* [*Copyright Tate Gallery, London, reprinted with permission.*]

Coldstream might not create a portrait of Melanie Klein "significant for those who never knew her", since neither painting, she thought, "conveyed a likeness to anyone—only a misty impression of such a head. No definite features or characteristic expression" (Stonebridge, 2007, pp. 110, 111). Riviere's doubts may be partly justified in relation to *Man with a Beard* where, as the title implies, Coldstream may have been more interested in a "type" rather than a real person, although the subject, Mr Wall, was indeed a real person and had sat for Coldstream on many occasions. Her criticisms, however, are difficult to sustain in front of the second painting, *Havildar Ajmer Singh*. The subject of the painting, Ajmer Singh, was a sergeant in the 2nd/11th Sikh regiment. Coldstream was captivated by the young man, noting in a letter to

Figure 46 *Havildar Ajmer Singh* (1943). *William Coldstream.* [*Copyright Tate Gallery, London, reprinted with permission.*]

Enid Canning, a close friend, that he was "28, in the army since he was 17—unmarried—about 6ft 2inches—very thin with the strange almost floating beard that young Sikhs have like dark ferns in water" (Laughton, 2004, p. 87). The painting dates from 1943, just after the allied victory at El Alamein, when Coldstream, in his role as official portrait painter to the War Office, and Ajmer Singh were both stationed in the army barracks at Mera, just outside Cairo. The portrait is Coldstream's best-known wartime painting and glows with the intense heat and sunlight of Egypt. In the words of Bruce Laughton, Coldstream's biographer, "the magnificent head is fixed firmly as a rock in its proportions" (Laughton, 2004, p. 86), and the soldier's "saffron yellow turban glows out of the darkness of the brownish-green shadows around it" (Laughton, 2004, p. 87). Coldstream had arrived in Egypt in a distraught state following a painful divorce after seven years of marriage to Nancy Sharp, a fellow artist at the Slade. In the warmth of the Mediterranean while occupied with this portrait, "his terrible feelings of despair experienced during his last year in London began to wash away" (Laughton, 2004, p. 85). The painting remained unfinished after Ajmer Singh's regiment was moved to a different location, and Coldstream was later to learn that Ajmer Singh himself had been seriously wounded in action during the battle for Monte Casino in Italy.

Apart from the issue of a physical likeness, Joan Riviere's other main concern, in her discussions with Stokes, was how Klein's professional colleagues might react to the painting. It was hoped that the portrait would hang in the Institute of Psychoanalysis in London, but Riviere foresaw difficulties. She explained to Stokes:

> There are a large contingent of members, mainly headed by Anna Freud . . . who do not support Mrs. Klein's work and are very jealous of her reputation and results. The Council and Officers of the Society are always at pains to show no partiality. . . . The suggestion was made that if the portrait were presented to Mrs. Klein, she might leave it in her will to the Institute. [Stonebridge, 2007, p. 111]

Even if the creation of the portrait was brought to a successful conclusion, what would become of it was unclear. For Riviere, the quest for an acceptable likeness and the politics of the portrait were key related issues.

The first sitting for the portrait was in March 1952. The dynamic between artist and subject was quite different from that which had existed between Melanie Klein and Oscar Nemon. Coldstream, aged 44, was an influential member of the arts establishment, and his artistic reputation was assured. Klein was older and had begun, as Grosskurth delicately phrases it, "to be poignantly aware of her own mortality" (Grosskurth, 1985, p. 392). Chezkel Zvi Kloetzel, with whom Melanie had a brief love affair in Berlin before she moved to London in 1926, had died in Jerusalem in October 1951. She had recently developed arthritis in her hip and now walked with a cane; and her friends had noticed that she tired easily. Michael Balint, a fellow psychoanalyst, observed in a letter to his family in Paris, "she [Melanie Klein] was old, tired and weak" (Dupont, 2002, p. 369). Indeed, a year later, in spring 1953, Klein was admitted to hospital for the investigation of dizzy spells and, following this, significantly reduced her clinical commitments, moving out of Clifton Hill because she was no longer able to manage the stairs.

Predictably, progress on the portrait was slow. At the end of May, after eighteen sittings, the unfinished portrait was seen by Coldstream's friend and fellow artist at the Slade, William Townsend, who wrote in his journal that "It looks as though it should be one of his best—the best for a long time" (Laughton, 2004, p. 170). The painstaking work continued, but in August, just before Klein left London for her annual holiday, the simmering dissatisfaction with the portrait came to a head. Joan Riviere wrote to Adrian Stokes with serious reservations, and Klein asked Stokes to explain the difficulties and problems, as she and her friends saw them, to Coldstream. In a detailed, anguished letter to his friend, Adrian Stokes summarised the objections. Klein, he wrote, "now puts far more store on the existence of a portrait of her than she did originally", and "everyone sees in the portrait a strong & formidable work of art in the making", but the very "definiteness" of the portrait is a source of much concern. Specifically, he said, Klein looks twenty years too old, and "the repose is the lethargy of extreme old age". More importantly, it makes Klein look "hard and unfeminine, not to say masculine". He recounted how the unfinished portrait was a source of great resentment to her friends because the image ignores Klein's "quick sympathy, warm-bloodedness & warm heart & a certain gaiety" (Sayers, 2012, p. 120). He thought it would inevitably play into the hands of her enemies, who accuse her, quite unjustly in his opinion, of being melancholic. In that context, he wonders whether it is "a fair exhibit to hand to posterity". Apparently Klein had suggested that a change in pose or clothes might help the situation, but, knowing his friend's working methods, Stokes confirmed he made clear to Klein that this was out of the question. Stokes asked Coldstream if he felt able to reassure Klein on these matters; but, with great sorrow, he advised abandoning the project if that were not possible. He concluded with profound apologies for writing such a wretched letter and said that, in his opinion, the portrait was a "very fine & powerful piece of work", and even Klein herself knew that the portrait she already had, referring to the one painted by Olga Dormandi, "is absolutely nothing beside yours" (Sayers, 2012, p. 120).

Klein and Coldstream discussed the matter in a telephone conversation. Coldstream said he was unable to give her any reassurance on how the painting would progress if he were allowed to continue and later confided to Townsend, "Melanie Klein would not give him any further sittings as she felt it made her look too old, serious and insufficiently feminine and he could not promise that more femininity would become apparent as the work progressed" (Laughton, 2004, p.170). Townsend commented in his journal, "as a psychologist she [Klein] could not see herself as others saw her. Bill very disappointed" (Laughton, 2004, p.170). In September, Klein wrote to Stokes, "I have returned from a very good holiday and feel much better for it" (Sayers, 2012, p. 122). In contrast to Klein's restored vitality, the following month, Coldstream's health was causing concern to his colleagues at the Slade: he was exhausted, tired, and overwrought (Laughton, 2004, p. 170). Conciliatory and consensual, Coldstream does not appear to have made any serious attempt to defend his painting or to argue its merits. Though his "powers of persuasion in committee work enabled him to win over the great and the good" (Sylvestor, 1987, p. 25), he appears to have meekly acquiesced to Klein's insistence that work on the portrait must be abandoned.

Adrian Stokes paid Coldstream for the unfinished portrait, which remained, however, at Klein's house. Coldstream had reassured Klein in their telephone conversation that he would remove the picture, but he did not do so. Klein wondered "whether he finds it too difficult to come to my house again" (Sayers, 2012, p. 122), but it is more probable that, having been paid for the work, Coldstream no longer considered it as his responsibility. Since he only painted from life—"I lose interest unless I let myself be ruled by what I see" (Coldstream, 1938, p. 104)—he would not have been motivated to work any further on the portrait. Klein was disturbed by the continued presence of the portrait in her house, and she wrote to Stokes in September, asking him to intervene with Coldstream and arrange for its removal (Sayers, 2012, p. 122). Ever mindful of his analyst's needs, Stokes eventually removed the portrait himself, taking it to his own home. A few weeks later, in early October, Klein invited

Stokes, his wife Ann, and Coldstream to take tea with her (Sayers, 2012, p. 123); no record of the conversation that afternoon survives.

In the same way that the Sutherland portrait, despite being hidden from view, had seemed to persecute Churchill, so Klein's image in the Coldstream painting, even though it was no longer in her house, continued to prey on her mind. In December 1952, she wrote to Stokes, asking him to destroy it. Klein appreciated that this was a difficult matter and felt uncomfortable about making such a request, because "I know it is a work of art and I hate the thought of having it destroyed". Nevertheless, she continued,

> My family and friends do not wish me to be perpetuated by this portrait. Moreover I am aware that people who have never seen me have a very phantastic conception of me as a person in connection with my work, and I certainly would not wish to add to this by leaving behind a painting which confirms it. [Sayers, 2012, p. 123]

Stokes did not carry out Klein's instructions, and two years later William Townsend saw the unfinished portrait again, describing it as "austere indeed, but majestic, beautifully drawn" (Laughton, 2004, p. 170). Stokes and Klein also viewed the portrait together that same year, when Stokes led Klein to believe that he no longer had any strong feelings about its destruction. In response to a direct question about whether she still wished the portrait to be destroyed, Klein replied in a letter written in July 1954 with an unequivocal yes: "I still feel about it as I did when I saw it first, that whatever its artistic value—it is a bad record of me and that I would not wish to be perpetuated like that" (Sayers, 2012, p. 124). Klein was, however, unwilling to accept personal responsibility for destroying the painting, leaving this for Stokes to do on her behalf. Torn between his desire to honour his analyst's feelings and his respect for a notable, if incomplete, work of art, Stokes was unable to act, eventually asking his wife to burn the painting while he was out of the house (Sayers, 2015a, p. 1020).

Ann Stokes [1922–2014] vividly describes destroying the painting in a recorded interview (Stokes, 2019). The act of burning the painting she found an "awful" and "a dreadful thing to do". She remembered Klein as a woman who "knew what she wanted. . . . [A] very handsome woman

Figure 47 Melanie Klein, aged 70 (1952). *William Coldstream (photograph of the unfinished painting, taken by Ann Stokes).* [*Copyright Bridgeman Images for the estate of Sir William Coldstream, reprinted with the kind permission of Philip Stokes.*]

. . . quite small and tubby but with a big head, a terrific head". But she was "too egotistical to realize it [the portrait] was good". In Ann's view, if Klein wanted the portrait destroyed, she should have done it herself, not used her influence over Adrian to compel him to take responsibility for its destruction. Before burning the painting, Ann took a black-and-white photograph, the only surviving representation of the painting (Figure 47). Afterwards, Ann and Adrian Stokes seem to have agreed to be evasive about the painting's fate, and, if asked, they planned to say that it had been sent to America. It was only when directly confronted by Bruce Laughton, during the research for his biography of Coldstream, that they confirmed the painting had indeed been destroyed (Laughton, 2004, p. 170).

The experience of working with Melanie Klein affected Coldstream's relationships with his subsequent sitters. His next portrait commission, which he accepted only with some reluctance, was the Right Reverend George Bell, Bishop of Chichester, an energetic church reformer interested in youth unemployment and social problems. Coldstream warned Bell before starting the painting that "It will drag on and no one will like it when it's done" (Laughton, 2004, p. 172). Just as he had predicted, reception of the painting was unenthusiastic: at the unveiling there was hesitant, half-hearted applause, and some described Bell as looking more like a boxer than a Bishop (Laughton, 2004, p. 174). Coldstream again deferred to the public reaction: he did not charge for the painting, which was hung only for a short while in the Church Commissioners' Offices before being quietly donated to the nation. Adrian Stokes, for his part, was left feeling guilty about the entire portrait fiasco, and, perhaps to compensate, he commissioned a painting of a nude from Coldstream (*Seated Nude, Miss Mond, 1952–1953; Tate Collection*), and later, in 1960, bought a second painting from the artist (*Seated Nude, Monica Hoye; 1959–1960; Private Collection*), which he displayed in his sitting room for many years afterwards. He wrote to Coldstream:

"Dear Bill, I must write a note to say how deeply happy and astonished I am to have this superb new painting. I wouldn't have conceived it possible that I should feel that it outstrips entirely the older one that I love so much. It sounds and re-sounds to me all the time the note of a very great masterpiece with an effect on me of utter gaiety, and I can think of no nude anywhere with which I would exchange it. . . . It moves me very deeply that you have let me have it and I cannot thank you enough." [Laughton, 2004, p. 205]

In 1954, the same year as the portrait of Klein was destroyed, Stokes gave Klein one of his own landscape paintings, a bland study in green of leafy trees in full summer. Klein was delighted with the gift: "It hangs opposite my analytic chair and I very much enjoy looking at it. It is an excellent painting and particularly appeals to me" (Sayers, 2012, p.124). During the course of an unpublished interview many years later, after Klein's death, Adrian Stokes revealed, in surprisingly bitter tones, his disillusionment with psychoanalysts and their view of art:

I am waging war with the psychoanalyst's approach to art. They don't understand it. Freud didn't understand it. He understood the artists perhaps as a clinical case but he did not appreciate painting. [Read, 2002, p. 238]

The photograph taken by Ann Stokes of the unfinished portrait shows a three-quarter-length image of Klein with her head resting on the back of a chair and hands folded in her lap. The body appears rather stiff and rigid, but the face is in repose, and she gazes into the middle distance. What was it exactly that Melanie Klein and her confidant Joan Riviere objected to? In a letter to Stokes written in September 1952, after her return from her summer holiday, Klein complained about the numerous sittings and enlisted the support of her doctor, Dame Annis Gillie, who, she said, was concerned about her rest at the weekends being disrupted so frequently (Sayers, 2012, p. 122). The specific reasons Klein gave for disliking the portrait were that Coldstream had made her look too old and serious and not sufficiently feminine (Laughton, 2004, p. 170). These are insubstantial and unsatisfactory explanations for Klein's response to the painting, and, as Stokes makes clear in his letter to Coldstream, there is more to this than "feminine vanity" (Sayers, 2012, p. 120). It is possible that Klein may have felt Coldstream was mocking her in some way (Sayers, 2015b, p. 224), perhaps stirring up feelings similar to those about the twice-life-sized Nemon bust. Bruce Laughton, in his biography of Coldstream, does report a disparaging anecdote, which Coldstream would apparently repeat to friends:

MK: "How much longer?"

WC: "It's just beginning to look human."

MK: "You can't tell whether it's a man or a woman."

WC: "But I said it's just beginning to look human." [Laughton, 2004, p. 170]

The anecdote circles in a telling way around the question of Klein's femininity. She must have had some formidable masculine qualities to have been able to hold her own in such a male-dominated world but was clearly not at ease with these, preferring, whenever possible, to emphasise her femininity (Steiner, personal communication,

2019). However that may be, and the story may well be apocryphal, it perhaps reflects more Coldstream's dismay at being prevented from finishing the portrait rather than his response to Klein while the work was in progress.

Riviere's attitude to the portrait was different, her tone more forthright, her verdict damning. Although she admired the unfinished work, writing to Adrian Stokes in August 1952 that she took the view that

The finished picture might possibly turn out to be a very great work of art, as portraying the nobility and tragedy in the human experience of acute depression, & in so doing could reveal the painter's talent as highly exceptional. [Stonebridge, 2007, p. 113]

But, she thought it "was a projection of unconscious experience in the painter, which may have its own independent value: as a portrait, however, it is a serious failure"—a failure because any portrait of Klein had "to be judged entirely on its merits as a portrait for posterity, as a likeness, and not as a work of art in itself". And this portrait completely failed that test. The painting did not do justice to Klein's "cheerfulness and gaiety" and her "immense vitality and elasticity" and, instead, portrayed her "in a state of static gloom", "isolated in suffering, withdrawn from life and all its interests & sunk in melancholic, not to say senile despair". The picture was a "ghastly caricature", which, if it were shown publicly, would cause "great offence" to Klein personally and "would not fail to damage her work and reputation".

The inevitable resistance to her work & its truths is weighty enough [but] untold damage would result if this presentation were allowed to become known as a view of her [because] opponents of her work have always regarded her views on the central importance of depression, & the persecution-phantasies, as evidence of personal psychotic tendencies in herself. [Stonebridge, 2007, p. 113]

Riviere was undoubtedly right that Coldstream's own psychology influenced his view of Klein. He had repeated episodes of depression throughout his life, which, by all accounts, he confronted with great courage (Ayer, 1987, p. 16). He was despairing when he arrived in Egypt in 1943 following his divorce, and in 1961 he had an acute breakdown during a committee meeting, when "he just locked up completely, became speechless" (Laughton, 2004, p. 208)—an internal conflict resolved only when he found the courage to propose to his model, Monica Hayer. But Riviere is surely wrong to insist that this is all a reflection of the artist's own inner world: Klein's melancholy was genuine and integral to her character, and, despite Coldstream's insistence that "when I am painting I make no conscious attempt to bring out the literary interest or character" (Coldstream, 1938, p. 103), he had clearly felt a profound sadness in Klein, which he was compelled to commit to canvas. The portrait had succeeded in revealing something authentic and very painful about herself, which Klein could not accept. For Riviere, the political impact of the portrait was paramount, overriding any concern for the merit of the painting as a work of art: this was a portrait for posterity, a portrait to promote Klein and her work, and only a particular likeness was acceptable. But for Klein, it was what the portrait confronted her with as an individual that lay at the heart of the problem. Melanie Klein was very consistent in her view, making it clear to Adrian Stokes on at least two occasions, in December 1952 and July 1954, that, whatever the merits of the painting, she did not want to be commemorated in that way (Sayers, 2012, pp. 123, 124): she wanted to be remembered as happy, vivacious, feminine, and motherly (Stokes, 2019). The unfinished portrait recalls, in its melancholic atmosphere and the refusal of Klein to engage with the viewer, the images of her youth and, in particular, the photograph by Aladár Székely. It was as if, by accepting the portrait's truth, Klein would somehow have conceded victory to the depression she had struggled with all her adult life.

Sad though the atmosphere of the portrait undoubtedly is, there is another, perhaps more positive and life-affirming sense in which Klein's abstraction, her reverie, can be understood. Is it not an image of an old lady reflecting on a long life, asking herself questions about her own self-worth: what damage had she done to her children, her family, her friends, what had she contributed, would her creative achievements help to repair and restore the hurt inflicted? Remembering, quietly and in repose, those she had lost, her sister Sidonie and, above all, her brother Emanuel, who, in one of his last letters to his sister, had pleaded with her, "Do not think ill of me because of my life, spread all the tolerance which could prepare you for your seventieth year on this my short life. I am not allowed to live till seventy, so permit me to invent it in poetry" (Grosskurth, 1985, p. 392). But, as in all such states, these thoughts may be swept away before you know it: a grandchild might run in, noisy, excited, full of the tumult of life, and Klein would be animated again, in the moment, enjoying and participating in the life and the exciting discoveries of a young child (Steiner, personal communication, 2019), the very thing that had absorbed her so passionately throughout her professional life.

The central creative tension at the heart of all portraiture—the conflict between the needs of the subject and the vision of the artist—had, unresolved, erupted and overwhelmed the endeavour. Unlike Olga Dormandi, Coldstream had failed in one of the key tasks of the portrait artist: he had been unable, had not even tried, to reconcile his artistic vision with the needs and wishes of his subject. Coldstream was the wrong artist at the wrong time; not allowed an artist's freedom to empathise with his subject, his honest approach was distrusted, and he was too naïve or too single-minded to negotiate with the powerful forces at work. All concerned—Klein, Riviere, and Stokes—agreed that the unfinished portrait was a good—even a great work of art—but Klein was too disturbed by the image to accept it and for this reason insisted on its destruction.

Four years later, in 1956, Stokes tried once more to interest Klein in a portrait, this time a sculpture by Sir Jacob Epstein. Klein was categorically dismissive:

> Your idea about the Epstein bust is in itself very attractive, but I would not in any circumstances permit people, even if they cared to do so, to spend such a lot of money for that purpose. [Sayers, 2012, p. 129]

* * *

In 1955 Klein established the Melanie Klein Trust, with some of her own money and the royalties from *New Directions in Psycho-Analysis* (Klein, Heimann, & Money-Kyrle, 1952). The initial trustees were Klein herself, Wilfred Bion, Paula Heimann, Betty Joseph, and Roger Money-Kyrle, and the aim was to further psychoanalytic research and teaching based on Klein's concepts. The new organisation was received with effusive praise by Ernest Jones, who, in the preface to the book, wrote:

> Mrs Klein's work of the past thirty years has been attacked and defended with almost equal vehemence. . . . It is a matter for wide satisfaction as well as for personal congratulations that Mrs Klein has lived to see her work firmly established. [Jones, 1955, p. v]

But no sooner was her recognition apparently secure than another crisis engulfed Klein, confusing her friends and supporters in London and causing bewilderment abroad. Since their original meeting shortly after the death of Klein's son Hans, Paula Heimann had been analysed by and become a close friend and an advocate of Klein's ideas, but growing personal and theoretical difficulties resulted in a painful break in November 1955. Klein wrote a brief, blunt letter to Heimann, demanding her resignation from the Trust:

> "This is a painful letter, so I shall make it short. I have been considering the Trust which has been formed to develop my work in the future. I have come to feel that I no longer have confidence in you as one of the people in whom I would wish to place such a trust. . . . I do not consider in a matter of such complexity that any purpose can be served by further personal discussion." [Grosskurth, 1985, p. 420]

The following few years were marred by bad-tempered arguments and struggles for power within the British Psychoanalytical Society centred on the training of candidates and their exposure to the different strands of theoretical thought within the Society, during which Klein defended her position trenchantly, making serious allegations of unfairness and patronage against the Council and Training Committee (Grosskurth, 1985, p. 431). Throughout this ongoing professional turbulence, Klein remained devoted to her three grandchildren, Michael, Diana, and Hazel; perhaps not the best mother herself, she was kind and patient with them and would, as they became older, take them on holiday in the summer, to the Rhine Valley and the Dolomites. This period of her life, after she moved out of the house in Clifton Hill to the flat in Bracknell Gardens in 1953, was perhaps the happiest of her life. Miss Cutler, her housekeeper, recalls constant entertaining, a hectic atmosphere, and a flat filled with young people (Grosskurth, 1985, p. 437). The year 1957 marked Klein's 75th birthday and was another year for commemoration. She was presented with a pen-and-gouache drawing of herself by Felix Topolski and was photographed by fellow psychoanalyst and former analysand, Dr Hans Thorner.

The extraordinary and prolific art of Feliks Topolski [1907–1989] chronicles the twentieth century in all its grotesque variety and wretched horror (Figure 48). Born in Warsaw to radical, atheist parents, he trained at the Warsaw Art Academy, encouraged and supported by his mother. His parents separated early in his childhood, and he saw little of his actor father, who died when Feliks was 18; his mother, who remarried, also died unexpectedly of complications during surgery, while Feliks was away from Warsaw, training on cavalry manoeuvres. 'Thus', as his son Daniel put it, "freed from family ties he embarked on a life dedicated to recording the seismic events that were to transform the twentieth century" (Topolski, 2010).

Topolski first came to the United Kingdom in 1935, working for many years in studios near Waterloo station. Trapped in London at the outbreak of war in 1939 and unable to rejoin his Polish regiment, he became, like William Coldstream, an official war artist, document-ing the Battle of Britain and the Arctic convoys to the Russian port of Archangel. After the war, he travelled widely, witnessing and drawing political events around the globe. Topolski had "a mania for drawing in action (never redrawing)", and "from an abundance of on-the-spot sketches" he would hand-print images "on rough brown butcher paper, using a printing press in his own studio" (Topolski, 2019). Many of these drawings were incorporated into the *Chronicles*, his attempt to bear witness to the current affairs of his time. Twenty-four issues a year, each devoted to a different subject, from 1953 to 1962, they contain in excess of 2,300 drawings. In the words of Harold Acton, he was "robust, cosmopolitan, mercurial, insatiable, witty with a gift for characterization expressed in a rapid, varied and individual vernacular". His imagination was "fertile and full of gusto", and he was constantly "recording impres-sions everywhere quick as thought". He seemed at one with his art: "he

Figure 48   Feliks Topolski (1954). *Edward Russell Westwood, London.* [*Copyright Russell Westwood Estate; National Portrait Gallery, London, reprinted with permission.*]

looks at life and lines flow from him with the spontaneity of speech" (Acton, 1951, pp. 4, 6).

Topolski drew Klein sometime in the mid-1950s, perhaps introduced to her by Hanna Segal, a fellow Pole (Grosskurth, 1985, p. 438); one of the sketches he made was presented to Klein at the 75th birthday party arranged by her friends at Bracknell Gardens. Topolski seems to have produced at least three different sketches (Figures 49 to 51), presumably all drawn at the same time, and it is not clear which version was given as a present. Interestingly, one of the sketches (Figure 50) seems to have vanished from the public realm, and the only evidence for its existence is as a black-and-white illustration on the dust jacket of one of the print

Figure 49   Melanie Klein, aged 75 (*c.*1957). *Feliks Topolski, London.* [*Copyright Hulton Archive / Getty Images, reprinted with permission.*]

runs for Phyllis Grosskurth's biography of Klein. All three sketches are characterised by Topolski's rapid pencil marks, which, although appearing perfunctory, subtly conjure up, through the varied weight and flow of the line, the outline of the head and the folds, creases, and shadows of the face, so that Klein's large head and grand hair emerge regal from the tangle of marks. In two versions (Figures 49 & 50), the right hand plays a prominent part, with Klein's chin resting on it in one, in a pose very similar to that chosen by Oscar Nemon, and, in the other, with an index finger extended imperiously from a jewelled hand, perhaps to emphasise a point she is making in discussion. In striking contrast to

Figure 50   Melanie Klein, aged 75 (*c.*1957). *Feliks Topolski, London.* [*Copyright Melanie Klein Trust, reprinted with permission.*]

the magisterial head, the hand and fingers are plump and stubby. Only in the third sketch (Figure 51), much softer and gentler than the other two, is Klein's age obvious. The mouth and eyes seem to recede, and the expression is restrained and wistful; as in many other similar images in this book, Klein is in half profile and looks away from the artist and away from us. Of Klein's reaction to the portraits there is no record, but her friends were divided in their opinion of the drawing presented as a birthday gift. Some were taken aback, feeling that Topolski had given Klein a "hawk-like appearance" (Grosskurth, 1985, p. 438), or "the look of a satiated vulture" (Kristeva, 2001, p. 210). Others, however, viewed it

Figure 51 Melanie Klein, aged 75 (c. 1957). *Feliks Topolski, London.* [*Copyright Alamy Images, reprinted with permission.*]

more positively: Hanna Segal thought it perfectly "captured the expression of satisfaction elicited when one has given a particularly perceptive interpretation" (Grosskurth, 1985, p. 438).

In a radio broadcast many years later, in 1983, Topolski recalls, just like Ann Stokes, how amazed he was by Klein's physical presence:

> She had this grand look and grooming and beauty. If I now recollect she was a large woman, with a large face and large features, but all regal indeed, not as our royals, there was great regality—No, regal as we imagine from fables. [Topolski, 1983]

On another occasion, he remembered her "arrogance and the rosy complexion of a Viennese woman fond of creamy pastries and conscious of her sex appeal" (Kristeva, 2001, p. 210). Interestingly, he had recalled Klein as tall and stately and was subsequently startled to learn that in fact she was not the tall woman of his memories (Grosskurth, 1985, p. 433).

Topolski's autobiography, *Fourteen Letters* (Topolski, 1988), is a stream-of-consciousness–like chronicle, without page numbering, recalling in its title the fourteen letters in his name, in which he makes some interesting observations about the process of portraiture and the subject's response to his or her portrait. He did not normally show the portrait to the sitter as it was being drawn, but, sooner or later, he writes, "the fateful confrontation would have to come". Despite the fact that Topolski's portrait sketches can often seem cruel and sadistic, only a few sitters reacted violently, and they, he observed, were usually the oldest. Like Adrian Stokes, he did not think this reaction was related to vanity but, rather, to the sudden confrontation with their own mortality. In his words, the subjects of a portrait have "a preserved/treasured mirror-view of themselves", they are "challenged by what to me was a living face, but to them the kept-at-bay face of disaster—in short the feared evocation of death". It is probably no coincidence that the two occasions when Klein destroyed the portraits created of her, the Nemon sculpture and the Coldstream painting, were also times associated with the deaths of significant individuals in her life. Oscar Nemon began his sculpture in the spring of 1939, and in August of that year Arthur Klein, Melanie's ex-husband, died in Switzerland. Arthur's sister, Jolan, travelled from Budapest for the funeral and was in frequent contact by letter and telephone with Melanie, who seems to have been distressed by his death (Grosskurth, 1985, p. 250). The other death was that of Klein's ex-lover, Chezkel Zvi Kloetzel, nine years younger than Melanie, who died in Palestine in the autumn of 1951, although Klein did not become aware of this until May 1952, while William Coldstream was working on her portrait. Eric, Klein's son, recalls how his mother appeared calm and unemotional when she told him the news, but that he later realised how much the relationship had meant to her (Grosskurth, 1985, p. 392).

Intimations of mortality and the desire for commemoration frequently go hand in hand, but, as Topolski realised, being brought face to face with your own mortality can be a shocking and painful experience. Unlike Coldstream and Nemon, who both acquiesced without a struggle to the destruction of their creations, Topolski was prepared to argue passionately for his art. When Edith Sitwell [1887–1964], poet and critic, objected to his portrayal of her as a crippled old lady, Topolski was mortified and replied with an eloquent letter defending his work and explaining that he had no intention to mock or caricature. "As an artist I am utterly SERIOUS in my work", he wrote (Topolski, 1988), going on to explain how sometimes the creative act of drawing felt to him like an unconscious process over which he had little control. Sitwell was moved by his generous letter and described how, on reflection, she had come to better understand her initial negative reaction to the painting, in which she is shown with a bent and stooped back. This, she now realised, had reminded her of a painful episode from her childhood when, at the insistence of her parents and doctors, she had been encased in a metal frame for eight years to try to straighten a spinal curvature. Sitwell invited Topolski to "come for sherry", and artist and author parted amicably, both enriched by the experience (Topolski, 2010).

Klein was commemorated on a second occasion in 1957, this time by her ex-analysand Hans Thorner [1905–1991]. Dr Thorner was born in Meissen and completed his medical training in Munich in 1930, where his skiing and alpine climbing companion, Rudolph Peierls, a nuclear physicist who later worked with Oppenheimer at Los Alamos, remembers that "he made a serious, almost gloomy first impression and talked slowly with a sonorous voice that showed interest and concern" (Peierls, 1985, p. 30). After qualifying, Thorner worked as a neurologist and psychiatrist in Frankfurt and Berlin, but he was dismissed from his post in May 1933 and classified as an enemy of the state by the National Socialists. He fled to Britain, later to discover that he had been identified as someone to be tracked down and arrested, should the Nazis ever invade England. In the late 1930s, he worked as Assistant Physician at the Peckham House mental hospital in South London and, during this period, started his analysis with Klein, later having a second analysis with Wilfred Bion. In the war years, with the rank of major in the British Army, he worked at Shenley psychiatric hospital in Hertfordshire. He later became a friend, translator, and supporter of Klein and a renowned teacher admired for the simplicity with which he conveyed complex psychoanalytic ideas (Shavit & Brenman-Pick, 2019). Thorner was an enthusiastic amateur photographer from his early days as a medical student; unlike Adrian Stokes, who commissioned a third party, William Coldstream, to commemorate his analyst for him, Thorner captured his own images of Klein (Figures 52 to 55).

The photographs taken by Thorner form the second of the three iconic sets of photographs made of Klein in her old age, the first by Douglas Glass and the final ones by Jane Bown. In the Thorner portraits there is not the same manipulation of lighting for effect as in the more professional images of Douglas Glass, but the setting is similar. His analyst sits in her consulting room; with a bookcase in the background and with the addition of an open book in her lap, the setting is studious and restrained. The swept-up hair gives the head a grand, stately appearance, and, although her presentation is less contrived than in the Glass portraits, Klein wears the same pearl earrings and necklace. Four separate photographs taken by Hans Thorner are preserved; two have been widely used and are well-known images of Klein, the other two are seldom seen. In the first (Figure 52), Klein sits in a small chair in front of a window; the lighting of the photograph recalls the painting by Olga Dormandi, with sunlight pouring through the window behind, but Klein seems diminished and shrunken, anxious perhaps, tense, and leaning slightly forward in the chair. The back lighting detracts from the grandeur of the head, and attention is drawn to the lines of age on her hands, which hold her reading glasses in her lap. In the second photograph (Figure 53), her position in the room has changed, she is more relaxed, and the face is open with a half-smile. The altered lighting, the angled shoulders, and the closer focus all help to bring the emphasis back to her head and features, Klein is no longer an old lady sitting in a chair: something more powerful begins to emerge. The remaining two photographs are remarkable and could not be more different, neatly encapsulating the polarised way in which Klein was viewed by

Figure 52   Melanie Klein, aged 75 (1957). *Hans Thorner, London. [Copyright Melanie Klein Trust, reprinted with permission.]*

the world. The first (Figure 54) recalls the more light-hearted images captured by Douglas Glass and the drawings by Topolski, relaxed, full of cheerfulness and gaiety. Jean MacGibbon, an early feminist, novelist, and critic, who was analysed by Melanie Klein following a serious mental breakdown at the end of the war, would describe this characteristic expression of Klein's as "an effervescent half chuckle that bubbles up in conversation" (MacGibbon, 1960). By contrast, in the second image (Figure 55) the liveliness has gone, and we are again confronted by the direct, uncompromising gaze that characterised the portrait from 1927 by Herbert Lambert; the eyes are steadfast, the mouth is set, and the chin

Figure 53 Melanie Klein, aged 75 (1957). *Hans Thorner, London.* [*Copyright Melanie Klein Trust, reprinted with permission.*]

is formidable, a face without illusions. It is the perfect pictorial representation of what Adrian Stokes would describe as Klein's "lonely and intellectual power" (Stokes, 1960). Hans Thorner later emphasised in an interview, long after Klein's death, her femininity; he appreciated her as a woman and what she had brought to psychoanalysis as a woman, but he also, like Adrian Stokes, felt a sense of isolation and loneliness.

> There was something kind of reticent that she wouldn't like to talk about herself. She was at the end a very lonely person, and she often complained that people were afraid to invite her. She would like to mix with people. [Thorner, 1983]

Figure 54 Melanie Klein, aged 75 (1957). *Hans Thorner, London. [Copyright Melanie Klein Trust, reprinted with permission.]*

* * *

Controversy, bitterness, and division pursued Klein into the last years of her life. In 1958, writing to her Swiss friend and colleague, Marcelle Spira, Klein reflected on her current position in the British Society.

> I myself have experienced so much isolation that I can fully sympathise with your position. Even now, when I have a number of capable and reliable colleagues to share my work, the feeling of isolation has by no means gone. In a society where I have worked for 32 years, I can still find a striking lack of understanding and good-will in the majority of colleagues. [Quinodoz, 2015, p. 92]

The extraordinary polarisation of views about her persisted, with negative opinions expressed in forthright and often intemperate language. R. D. Laing, in the course of his training, attended Klein's clinical and theoretical seminars (Grosskurth, 1985, p. 446), and, although he had respect for her ideas and the depth of her sensibility, in a later interview he stated bluntly that he found her "an absolutely detestable person" characterised by "adamantine dogmatism" whose followers were "beaten

Figure 55 Melanie Klein, aged 75 (1957). *Hans Thorner, London.* [*Copyright Melanie Klein Trust, reprinted with permission.*]

down into complete submission" (Grosskurth, 1985, p. 446). Others criticised the Kleinians, as they were now known, for lacking humour: A. S. Neill, headmaster of the progressive school Summerhill, said of them, "they can't laugh; Melanie has evidently shown them humour is a complex which no normal man should have" (Grosskurth, 1985, p. 448). But others found her gentle and totally unpersecuting in supervision, patient, kind, courteous, straightforward and clear, with a fine sensitivity in listening and a remarkable memory. In direct contrast to the views of Laing, she is remembered as someone who laid great stress on respecting the scientific integrity of others, even though they may have had views divergent from her own, which she acknowledged herself, "perhaps because I know only too well how hard it is, and have been myself swept by passionate feelings and at certain moments needed unconditional support" (Grosskurth, 1985, p. 446).

It was on loneliness that Klein made her final contribution, delivering her paper "On the Sense of Loneliness" to the International Congress in Copenhagen in July 1959. She spoke about an inner sense of loneliness, the sense of being alone regardless of external circumstances, of feeling lonely even among loving friends or when receiving love, and she drew on her deepest experiences of grief, depression, and loneliness itself. She thought that this internal loneliness arose from a ubiquitous yearning for an unattainable perfect internal state, and that, however gratifying it is to share thoughts and feelings with a congenial person, there always remains an unsatisfied longing for an understanding without words, ultimately for the earliest relationship with one's mother, which is irretrievably lost (Klein, 1963, pp. 300, 301).

The final images of Klein were taken in July 1959, at the time of the Copenhagen Congress and a year before her death in September 1960. They were captured by Jane Bown [1925–2014], an English portrait photographer (Figure 56), who for many years worked on the *Observer* newspaper, where she was known as the "white witch for her uncanny ability to capture, time and again, a psychologically insightful portrait" (Dodd & McCabe, 2014). Born in Dorset and small in stature like Klein, Bown spoke with a clipped, "posh" accent. A seemingly happy childhood, when she was looked after by a series of "aunts", was shattered when, aged 12, she discovered that one of the "aunts" was, in fact, her real mother, who had become pregnant while nursing a dying patient, her father. The deception about her birth scarred her deeply, and the hurt remained alive into her old age (Dodd & McCabe, 2014). She felt a profound, lifelong sense of not belonging and always sought anonymity (Dodd, 2015, p. 11). "As a teenager she would latch herself onto families; in her early pictures many seemingly happy families are viewed sideways or from behind" (Dodd & McCabe, 2014). Bown was "happiest mooching about", and, "right to the end of her working life, she liked nothing better than prowling around a train station, a small, unobtrusive figure

Figure 56   Jane Bown (1986). *Yevonde Middleton, London.* [*Copyright Yevonde Portrait Archive/Mary Evans Picture Library, reprinted with permission.*]

with an Olympus OMI navigating the waves of commuters, unseen and observant" (Dodd, 2015, p. 7). She aimed for spontaneity in her portraits, working quickly, with "simple equipment and no tricks" (Bown, 2000, p. 6). She said of photography, "I don't make pictures, I try and find them" (Bown, 2000, p. 9). Her professional break came in 1949, when she was told to go and photograph Bertrand Russell for the newspaper; she recalls that the shoot was "a horror story, I didn't even think I knew who he was", "but the light was good" (Dodd, 2015, p. 8). In the words of Luke Dodd, her editor, although she photographed the great and the famous, she was most drawn to people on the margins of society and captured them with "profound humanity and lack of sentimentality" (Dodd, 2015, p. 11).

> She wasn't interested in action, what motivated her was quietness, the point when all the noise and bluster has stopped or moved on [hers was a] fundamentally melancholic nature, sadness and doubt infuse her most memorable work. [Dodd, 2015, p. 13]

Jane Bown was a young woman of 35, early in her career, when she took these beautiful images (Figures 57 to 59) of Klein in old age, in her sitting room at Bracknell Gardens. Integral to their appeal is their enigmatic nature and their wonderful grace and softness, recalling the images taken in 1944 by Bertl Sachsel. There is again a backdrop of books, and Klein, for the first time since early childhood in a portrait photograph, wears a floral-patterned dress, with necklace and earrings. Natural light is used to great effect to delineate the structure of the face, and the portrait in full profile, in particular (Figure 57), makes manifest the regality that had been commented on so frequently in the past. In the other two portraits (Figures 58 & 59), although Klein's gaze is still averted, it is not sealed off, not hermetically closed, as in many of the other portraits; on the contrary, she seems to invite us in, encouraging, wanting us to share. Klein is vigilant, hesitant certainly, perhaps a little wary, but there is, nevertheless, a clear sense of trust and recognition between subject and artist, an obvious empathy (Dodd, 2015, p. 17). When Jane Bown "looked through a lens, in that charged moment that she always characterised in terms of love, she made the world into a place that was utterly and unmistakably her own" (Dodd, 2015, p. 14). The truth of these words clearly applies to Jane Bown's photographs of Melanie Klein, portraits in which she successfully achieved a synthesis that many of the other artists who worked with Klein struggled to approach.

Phyllis Grosskurth reports that in the last year of her life: "Klein asked Jean MacGibbon with almost a hint of wistfulness, 'Couldn't you call me Melanie?' to which MacGibbon is said to have replied, 'Oh no, Mrs Klein, I couldn't possibly!'" (Grosskurth, 1985, p. 455). Jean Mac-Gibbon thought that many people saw Melanie Klein as "a kind of ideal

Figure 57 Melanie Klein, aged 77 (1959). *Jane Bown, London. [Copyright Melanie Klein Trust, reprinted with permission.]*

mother—her genius, her beauty, her presence—and as a result she must have felt a little lonely and distanced from intimacy" (Grosskurth, 1985, p. 455). A loving and doting grandmother, Klein would have been fully aware that, as a mother herself, she had "lost" two of her three children: one son had died, and her daughter was permanently estranged from her. She, of all people, would have understood what it was to be a good mother and would, no doubt, have desperately liked to be one; this was, perhaps, the source of her desire always to be portrayed as warm, nurturing, accepting, forgiving, and generous. It cannot therefore be a coincidence that the three artists who produced the most sympathetic

Figure 58 Melanie Klein, aged 77 (1959). *Jane Bown, London. [Copyright Melanie Klein Trust, reprinted with permission.]*

portraits of Klein were all women, all, in their own way, motherless. Bertl Sachsel had left her family in Germany, many of whom were to die in the Holocaust, when she fled to England in the early 1930s and gave birth in 1944 to her son, the year she took her photographs of Klein; Olga Dormandi had been cruelly separated from her mother, Vilma, for many years in early childhood and then, when she fled with her husband and daughter to Paris, had left her mother behind in Budapest, where she died shortly afterwards; and, finally, Jane Bown, cold and bitter towards her own mother for the catastrophic deception about her birth, was just starting out on her career and recently married, with a young

Figure 59   Melanie Klein, aged 77 (1959). *Jane Bown, London. [Copyright Melanie Klein Trust, reprinted with permission.]*

child, when she photographed Klein. Some, at least, of the male artists were able to empathise with Klein's depression and sadness, but it was the women who identified with the bereft mother.

A year later, in May 1960, Melanie Klein was interviewed by Jean MacGibbon. These months were dominated for Klein by severe exhaustion, due, it transpired, to progressive anaemia. The interview was originally intended to appear in the *Observer*, but the editor, David Astor, who had been analysed by Anna Freud, refused to publish it (Grosskurth, 1985, p. 454). Always alert to what was said about her in print, just as she had been about the images made of her in past years,

Klein went to see MacGibbon while she was writing up the interview "to make sure that my account of her work was accurate, my impression of herself, not too wide of the mark" (Grosskurth, 1985, p. 454). In the event, Klein was very pleased with the review and wrote to MacGibbon to thank her in words that were "characteristically unassuming, straightforward, warmhearted" (Grosskurth, 1985, p. 454). In the piece, which was eventually published in the *Guardian*, MacGibbon wrote:

> Mrs Klein is one of the fortunate few who seem not to age in any ordinary sense but, endowed with an extraordinary vitality, go on developing throughout their entire lifespan. . . . About her femininity and delicate mobile features there is no sense of preservation; and in talk there is no barrier of age, but a direct and open understanding, a relevance clear and considered, expressed with an unassuming and spontaneous humour that makes for the most stimulating of companions. [MacGibbon, 1960]

By now frail and ill, that summer Klein travelled, with her grandson Michael, to Switzerland, hoping once more that the mountains and the fresh air would revive her; but at Villars-sur-Ollon, where she was joined by her son Eric, she became dangerously ill and had to be flown back to London. Cancer of the colon was diagnosed, and, despite surgery, she died of complications on the 22nd of September. To her distraught grandson, Michael, she said that

> She was not afraid of death. The only thing that was immortal was what one had achieved; and her strength and courage lay in her belief that one's ideas were carried forward by others. [Grosskurth, 1985, p. 461]

REFERENCES

Abel-Hirsch, N. (2019). *Bion: 365 Quotes.* London: Routledge.

Acton, H. (1951). Introduction. In: Feliks Topolski, *88 Pictures.* London: Methuen.

Ayer, A. (1987). Contribution. In: *William Coldstream Memorial Meeting, 24th April 1987.* London: University College.

Balint, M. (1952). New beginning and the paranoid and the depressive syndromes. *International Journal of Psychoanalysis, 33*: 214–224.

Bell, A. O. (Ed.) (1984). *The Diary of Virginia Woolf, Volume 5: 1936–41.* London: Penguin.

Bell, G. (1939). *The Artist and His Public.* London: Hogarth Press.

Bown, J. (2000). *Faces: The Creative Process Behind Great Portraits.* London: Collins & Brown.

Brimblecombe, D. (2011). Personal communication, Diana Brimblecombe to Aurelia Young.

Brimblecombe, D., & Bentall, H. (2014). *Melanie Klein Was Our Granny: A Conversation with Melanie Klein's Granddaughters* [Video]. London: Melanie Klein Trust. <www.melanie-klein-trust.org.uk/audiovisual> (last accessed 16 April 2019).

Bynum, H. (2012). *Spitting Blood: The History of Tuberculosis.* Oxford: Oxford University Press.

Carroll, H. (2015). *Read This If You Want to Take Great Photographs of People.* London: Lawrence King.

Coldstream, W. (1938). Painting. In: R. S. Lambert (Ed.), *Art in England* (pp. 99–104). London: Pelican.

Dodd, L. (2014). *Jane Bown: Turning the Lens on Britain's Shyest Photographer. The Guardian*, London, 24 April.

Dodd, L. (2015). *Jane Bown: A Lifetime of Looking.* London: Faber.

Dodd, L., & McCabe, E. (2014). *Jane Bown Obituary. The Guardian*, London: 21 December. <https://www.theguardian.com/artanddesign/2014/dec/21/jane-bown> (last accessed 20 April 2019).

Dormandi, O. (2019). *Olga Dormandi* [Biography]. In: <https://www.olga-dormandi.com/en/home> (last accessed 10 April 2019).

Dubos, R., & Dubos, J. (1996). *The White Plague: Tuberculosis, Man and Society.* Boston, MA: Rutgers University Press.

Dupont, J. (2002). Excerpts of the correspondence of Michael and Alice Balint with Olga, Ladislas and Judith Dormandi. *American Journal of Psychoanalysis, 62* (4): 359–381.

Dupont, J. (2013). Ferenczi at Maresfield Gardens. *American Journal of Psychoanalysis, 73* (1): 1–7.

Félszeghy, I. (2019). *Women Psychoanalysts in Hungary: Ilona Felszeghy* [Biography]. <https://www.psychoanalytikerinnen.de/hungary_biographies.html#Felszeghy> (last accessed 19 April 2019).

Fletcher, J. (2008). The Renaissance portrait: Functions, uses and display. In: L. Campbell, M. Falomir, J. Fletcher, & L. Syson (Eds.), *Renaissance Faces: Van Eyck to Titian* (pp. 46–65). London: National Gallery.

Freud, S. (1901). *On Dreams. Standard Edition, Vol. 5.* London: Hogarth Press, 1953.

Freud Museum (2018). *Sándor Ferenczi's Archive.* London. <https://www.freud.org.uk/exhibitions/sandor-ferenczis-archive/> (last accessed 19 April 2019).

Furness, H. (2015). The secret of Winston Churchill's unpopular Sutherland portrait revealed. *The Daily Telegraph*, 10 July.

Gaye, B. (2019). *Gaye, Bertl* [Biography]. In: Fading Images <www.fadingimages.uk/photoGa.asp> (last accessed 16 April 2019).

Gowring, L. (1962). Introduction. In: Arts Council, *William Coldstream Exhibition Catalogue* (pp. 5–15). London: Arts Council of Great Britain.

Gowring, L. (1987). Introduction. In: *William Coldstream Memorial Meeting*, 24 April. London: University College.

Grosskurth, P. (1985). *Melanie Klein: Her World and Her Work*. London: Hodder & Stoughton.

Hughes, A. (1991). Joan Riviere: Her life and work. In: A. Hughes (Ed.), *The Inner World of Joan Riviere: Collected Papers 1920–1958* (pp. 1–44). London: Karnac.

Jaques, E. (1983). Contributor. In: R. Wollheim (Chair), *Melanie Klein*. BBC Radio 3, 12 July. <http://www.melanie-klein-trust.org.uk/domains/melanie-klein-trust.org.uk/local/media/downloads/BBC_Radio_Klein_1983_transcript.pdf>

Joffee Goodfriend, G. (1965). Her love of life is reflected on canvas. *Kansas City Times,* 29 October.

Jones, E. (1948). Introduction to *Contributions to Psychoanalysis 1921–45*. In: M. Klein, *Envy and Gratitude and Other Works 1946–1963* (pp. 337–340). London: Karnac, 1993.

Jones, E. (1952). Preface. In: M. Klein, P. Heimann, & R. E. Money-Kyrle (Eds.), *New Directions in Psycho-Analysis: The Significance of Infant Conflict in the Pattern of Adult Behaviour* (p. v). London: Karnac, 1993.

Jones, J. (2001). Winston Churchill & Graham Sutherland. *The Guardian*, 3 November.

King, P. (1989). Paula Heimann's quest for her own identity as a psychoanalyst: An introductory memoir. In: P. Heimann, *About Children and Children-No-Longer, Collected Papers 1942–80* (pp. 3–9), ed. M. Tonnesmann. London: Routledge.

Klein, M. (1929). Infantile anxiety situations reflected in a work of art and in the creative impulse. In: *Love, Guilt and Reparation and Other Works* (pp. 210–218). London: Hogarth Press, 1975.

Klein, M. (1932). *The Psycho-Analysis of Children*. London: Hogarth Press, 1975.

Klein, M. (1935). A contribution to the psychogenesis of manic-depressive states. In: *Love, Guilt and Reparation and Other Works 1921–1945* (pp. 262–289). London: Karnac: 1992.

Klein, M. (1936). Weaning. In: *Love, Guilt and Reparation and Other Works 1921–1945* (pp. 290–305). London: Karnac: 1992.

Klein, M. (1937). Love, guilt and reparation. In: *Love, Guilt and Reparation and Other Works 1921–1945* (pp. 306–343). London: Karnac: 1992.

Klein, M. (1939). *Melanie Klein Walking in the Garden* [Cine film]. London: Melanie Klein Trust. <www.melanie-klein-trust.org.uk/audiovisual> (last accessed 11 April 2019).

Klein, M. (1940). Mourning and its relation to manic-depressive states. In: *Love,*

Guilt and Reparation and Other Works 1921–1945 (pp. 344–369). London: Karnac: 1992.

Klein, M. (1963). On the sense of loneliness. In: *Envy and Gratitude and Other Works 1946–1963* (pp. 300–313). London: Karnac, 1993.

Klein, M., Heimann, P., & Money-Kyrle, R. E. (Eds.) (1952). *New Directions in Psycho-Analysis: The Significance of Infant Conflict in the Pattern of Adult Behaviour.* London: Karnac, 1993.

Kristeva, J. (2001). *Melanie Klein.* New York: Columbia University Press.

Lambert, H. (1923). *Modern British Composers: Seventeen Portraits.* London: F & B Goodwin.

Lambert, H. (1930). *Studio Portrait Lighting* (1st edition). London: Pitman.

Lampert, C. (1984). *William Coldstream: New Paintings.* London: Anthony d'Offay.

Lancaster, J. (2007). I knew Sir Winston well—Churchill and Oscar Nemon. *Finest Hour, 137*: 14–18.

Laughton, B. (2004). *William Coldstream.* New Haven, CT: Yale University Press.

Lawrence-Lightfoot, S., & Hoffman-Davis, J. (1997). *The Art and Science of Portraiture.* San Francisco, CA: Jossey-Bass.

Likierman, M. (2001). *Melanie Klein: Her Work in Context.* London: Continuum.

MacGibbon, J. (1960). Melanie Klein. *The Guardian*, 16 May.

McMullan, R. (2011). Personal communication, Robert McMullan to Aurelia Young.

Melanie Klein Trust (2016). Personal communication. Melanie Klein Trust to Aurelia Young.

Mellor, D. (1978). *Reflected Glory: Photographs by Douglas Glass* [Exhibition Catalogue]. London: South East Arts Association & Rye Art Gallery.

Molnar, M. (1992). *The Diary of Sigmund Freud, 1929–1939: A Chronicle of Events in the Last Decade.* London: Hogarth Press.

Nemon, O. (2019). *Oscar Nemon: Sculptor—1906–1985.* <https://www.oscar-nemon.org.uk/> (last accessed 11 April 2019).

Peierls, R. (1985). *Bird of Passage: Recollections of a Physicist.* Princeton, NJ: Princeton Legacy Library.

Pick, D., & Milton, J. (2001). *Memories of Melanie Klein: An Interview with Hanna Segal.* London: Melanie Klein Trust. <http://www.melanie-klein-trust.org.uk/domains/melanie-klein-trust.org.uk/local/media/downloads/Memories_of_Melanie_Klein_Hanna_Segal.pdf>

Quinodoz, J.-M. (2015). *Melanie Klein and Marcelle Spira: Their Correspondence and Context.* London: Routledge.

Read, R. (2002). *Art and Its Discontents: The Early Life of Adrian Stokes.* Aldershot: Ashgate.

Sayers, J. (2012). Dear Stokes: Letters from Melanie Klein about Writing, painting and psychoanalysis. *Psychoanalysis and History, 14* (1): 111–132.

Sayers, J. (2015a). Adrian Stokes and the portrait of Melanie Klein. *International Journal of Psychoanalysis, 96* (4): 1013–1024.

Sayers, J. (2015b). *Art, Psychoanalysis and Adrian Stokes: A Biography.* London: Routledge.

Sayers, J., & Forrester, J. (2013). The autobiography of Melanie Klein. *Psychoanalysis and History, 15* (2): 127–163.

Sebba, A. (2011). Discovering a father: Oscar Nemon and his daughter Aurelia. *The Times T2,* August. <http://annesebba.com/journalism/discovering-a-father-oscar-nemon-and-his-daughter-aurelia/> (last accessed 4 July 2017).

Segal, H. (1979). *Klein.* London: Karnac, 1989.

Segal, H. (1991). *Dream, Phantasy and Art.* London: Routledge.

Segal, H. (1998). A psychoanalytical approach to aesthetics. In: J. Phillips & L. Stonebridge (Eds.), *Reading Melanie Klein* (pp. 203–222). London: Routledge.

Shavit, N., & Brenman-Pick, I. *Hans Thorner.* London: Melanie Klein Trust. <http://www.melanie-klein-trust.org.uk/thorner> (last accessed 20 April 2019).

Sherwin-White, S. (2017). *Melanie Klein Revisited.* London: Karnac.

Soames, M. (1979). *Clementine Churchill.* London: Doubleday.

Steiner, J. (2019). Personal communication, John Steiner to Roger Amos, 27 February.

Stokes, A. (1932). *The Quattro Cento.* London: Faber & Faber.

Stokes, A. (1955). *Michelangelo: A Study in the Nature of Art.* London: Tavistock Press.

Stokes, A. (1960). Letter. *The Times,* 26 September.

Stokes, A. (1962). Coldstream and the sitter. In: The Arts Council, *William Coldstream Exhibition* (pp. 15–16). London: Arts Council of Great Britain.

Stokes, A. (2019). *British Library Sounds, No. 6 of 17: Stokes, Ann. National Life Stories Collection: Craft Lives.* <http://sounds.bl.uk/Oral-history/Crafts/021M-C0960X0013XX-0006V0> (last accessed 17 April 2019).

Stonebridge, L. (2007). Portrait of an analyst: Adrian Stokes and Melanie Klein. In: S. Bann (Ed.), *The Coral Mind: Adrian Stokes' Engagement with Architecture, Art History, Criticism and Psychoanalysis* (pp. 105–121). University Park, PA: Pennsylvania State University Press.

Stonebridge, L., & Phillips, J. (1998). Introduction. In: J. Phillips & L. Stonebridge (Eds.), *Reading Melanie Klein* (pp. 1–10). London: Routledge.

Sylvestor, D. (1987). Contributor. In: *William Coldstream: Memorial Meeting 24th April 1987*. London: University College.

Székely, A. (2019). *Aladar Szekely* [Biography]. <www.szekelyaladarfotoklub.hu/szekely-aladar> (last accessed 10 April 2019).

Thorner, H. (1983). Contributor. In: R. Wollheim (Chair), *Melanie Klein*. BBC Radio 3, London, 12 July. <http://www.melanie-klein-trust.org.uk/domains/melanie-klein-trust.org.uk/local/media/downloads/BBC_Radio_1983_Klein_transcript_accessible_version.pdf>

Topolski, D. (2010). *Feliks Topolski: Eyewitness to the Twentieth Century*. Lecture delivered at Gresham College, London, 22 March. <www.gresham.ac.uk/lectures-and-events/feliks-topolski-eye-witness-to-the-20th-century>

Topolski, F. (1983). Contributor. In: R. Wollheim (Chair), *Melanie Klein*. BBC Radio 3, London, 12 July. <http://www.melanie-klein-trust.org.uk/domains/melanie-klein-trust.org.uk/local/media/downloads/BBC_Radio_Klein_1983_transcript.pdf>

Topolski, F. (1988). *Fourteen Letters: An Autobiography*. London: Faber & Faber.

Topolski, F. (2019). *Topolski Century* [Biography]. London: Topolski Studio. <http://www.topolskicentury.org.uk/memoir> (last accessed 17 April 2019).

Toruk, M., Sylwan, B., & Covello, A. (1998). Melanie Mell by herself. In: J. Phillips & L. Stonebridge (Eds.), *Reading Melanie Klein* (pp. 51–80). London: Routledge.

Uglow, E. (1987). Contributor. In: *William Coldstream Memorial Meeting,* 24 April. London: University College.

Wakatsuki, J. (2019). *Jeanne Wakatsuki* [Biography]. <https://biography.jrank.org/pages/2134/Houston-Jeanne-Wakatsuki-1934.html> (last accessed 16 April 2019).

Wilde, O. (1985). *The Picture of Dorian Gray*. London: Penguin.

Wood, J. (2015). Oscar Nemon: "The Temple of Universal Ethics" (1938). In: *Sculptors' Papers from the Henry Moore Institute Archive,* pp. 13–16. Essays on Sculpture, No. 71. Leeds: Henry Moore Institute.

Young, A. (2017a). Personal communication. Aurelia Young to The Melanie Klein Trust, 15 February.

Young, A. (2017b). Personal communication. Aurelia Young to Roger Amos, 18 May 2017.

Young, A., & Hale J. (2018). *Finding Nemon*. London: Peter Owen.

INDEX

Abel-Hirsch, N., 11
Abraham, K., 4, 47, 49
Académie Royale des Beaux-Arts,
    Brussels, 56
Acton, H., 104, 105
Ady, E., 41, 42
Aksamovich, A., 56
Alberti, L. B., 5
Alexander, F., 49
Arts Council England, 86
Astor, D., 121
Austro-Hungarian Empire, 75
Ayer, A., 100

Balint, A., 49, 73, 75
Balint, M., 47, 49, 73, 75, 76, 93
Bell, A. O., 61
Bell, George, 98
Bell, Graham, 89
Bentall, H., 103
Berény, R., 47, 48, 74
Berlin, Melanie Klein in, 46–49

Berlin Psychoanalytical Society, 47, 49,
    54
Bion, W. R., 11, 102, 111
Bonaparte, M., 57, 75, 76
Borghese, D., 69
Bown, J., 111, 116–121
Brandes, G., 29
Brenman-Pick, I., 111
Brill, A., 57
Brimblecombe, D., 64, 66, 78, 103
British Film Institute, 86
British Psychoanalytical Society, 51,
    60–63, 70, 103, 114
Budapest, Melanie Klein in, 29–43,
    45–46
Bynum, H., 14

Canning, E., 92
Carpathian Mountains/Tatra
    Mountains, 4, 61
Carroll, H., 4
Central School of Art, London, 81

Cézanne, P., 47
child analysis, 45, 48, 54
Child Guidance Centre, Vienna, 49
childhood anxiety, 47
Churchill, C., 9, 10
Churchill, W., 9, 10, 60, 67, 96
Clark, K. M., Lord, 82
Clyne, M., 61, 103, 122
Coldstream, W., 5, 7, 8, 10, 11, 79, 81,
     85, 87–104, 109–111
Coldstream Reports, 86
Colette, S.-G., 10
"Controversial Discussions", 70
Covello, A., 29
Coventry Cathedral tapestry, 9
Croatia, 54, 59, 63

Deutsch, L., 13, 16, 32, 33
Deutsch-Kreutz (Burgenland), Austria,
     13
Dodd, L., 4, 116, 117, 118
Dormandi, A., 734
Dormandi, F., 73
Dormandi, L., 75
Dormandi, O., 8, 11, 16–18, 27, 48,
     73–79, 95, 102, 111, 120
Dormandi, V., 73, 75, 120
Dubos, J., 16
Dubos, R., 16
Dunky, F., 41
Dunky, K., 41
Dupont, J., née Dormandi, 73, 75, 76, 94

Eitingon, M., 58
El Alamein, 92
Elliot and Fry's Studio, London, 51, 55
Epstein, Sir J., 102
Euston Road School, London, 86, 89

Federn, P., 57–59, 66–67
Félszeghy, I., 75, 76
Ferenczi, S., 34, 35, 41, 45, 56, 61, 63,
     73, 75

Ferenczi Archive, Freud Museum,
     London, 76
Fichtl, P., 59
First World War, 19, 45, 75
     Treaty of Trianon, 46
Fletcher, J., 5
Forrester, J., 3, 4, 14, 16, 24, 25, 28, 29,
     32, 45
Freud, A., 51, 54, 63, 93, 121
     "Controversial Discussions", 70
Freud, S., 34, 35, 45, 47, 49, 51, 57–59,
     63, 67, 76, 99
Freud Museum, London, 59, 76
Furness, H., 9, 10

Gaye, A., 72
Gaye, F., 71
Gaye, B., 71, 72, 73
     see also Sachsel, B.
Genoa, Italy, 27, 28, 29, 32
Gillie, Dame A., 99
Glass, D., 81–86, 111, 112
Glover, E., 62
Gowring, L., 87, 88
Grosskurth, P., 2, 4, 5, 14, 16, 17, 22, 31,
     32, 35, 38, 40, 46, 47, 49, 60–65,
     81, 93, 102–109, 114–116, 118,
     119, 121, 122

Hale J., 9, 54, 56, 58, 59, 60, 63, 64, 67, 68
Hapsburg Court, 18
Hayer, M., 101
Hegedüs Studio, Budapest, 30–32
Heimann, P., 60, 61, 102, 103
Hoffman-Davis, J., 6
Holbein, H., 82
Holocaust, 59, 71, 120
Howells, H., 52, 53
Hug-Hellmuth, H., 49
Hughes, A., 90
Hungarian Psychoanalytical Society, 45,
     73, 75
Hungary, 41, 45–47, 73, 75

Institute of Psychoanalysis, London, 63, 93
International Ferenczi Center, 75
International Psychoanalytical Congresses:
  5th, Budapest, 1918, 45
  7th, Berlin, 1922, 47
  8th, Salzburg, 1924, 48
  21st, Copenhagen, 1959, 116
Isaacs, S., 60

Jaques, E., 2
Joffee Goodfriend, G., 78
Jones, J., 1, 9, 49, 57, 60, 63, 81, 103
Joseph, B., 102

Kempton, J., 68
King, P., 60, 61
Kjar, R., 10
Klein, A., 4, 23–26, 29, 30, 32, 33, 38, 46, 49, 109
Klein, E. [Eric Clyne], 4, 40, 46, 49, 61, 64, 109, 122
Klein, H., 4, 30, 31, 32, 33, 46, 61, 103
Klein, J., 109
Klein, Melanie (*passim*):
  Berlin, 46–49
  Budapest, 29–43, 45–46
  child analysis, 45, 48, 54
  "Controversial Discussions", 70
  depression, 3, 4, 9, 32, 40, 41, 61, 100, 101, 116, 121
  engagement, 26
  London, 51–79, 81–122
  marriage, 29–44
    attitude towards, 4
  personality, 2, 3, 4, 5, 8, 11, 62
  play technique, 1
  see also Reizes, M.
Klein, Melitta, *see* Schmideberg, M.
Kloetzel, C. Z., 47, 61, 93, 109
Koch, R., 14
Kokoschka, O., 56

Kovács, F., 73
Krappitz, Upper Silesia, 30, 31
Kristeva, J., 107, 109
Kun, B., 45

Laforgue, R., 9, 57, 66
Laing, R. D., 114, 115
Lambert, H., 51–55, 71, 112
Lampert, C., 88
Lane, S., 68
Laughton, B., 85, 87, 88, 92–99, 101
Lawrence-Lightfoot, S., 6
Lemburg (Lvov), Galicia, 13
Likierman, M., 2
London, Melanie Klein in, 51–79, 81–122
London Institute of Psychoanalysis, 63
lung cancer, 16

MacGibbon, J., 112, 118, 121, 122
Mahler, G., 56
McCabe, E., 116
McMullan, R., 63
Medical University of Vienna, 59
Melanie Klein Trust, 64, 68, 69, 102
Mellor, D., 82
Menuhin, Y., 72
Meštrović, I., 56
Middleton, Y. [Madame Yevonde], 117
Milner, M., 76
Milton, J., 2
Miró, J., 82
Molnar, M., 59
Money-Kyrle, R. E., 102
Mozart, W. A., 72

National Advisory Council on Arts Education, 86
National Gallery, London, 86
National Socialism/Nazism, 75, 110
  Holocaust under, 59, 72, 120
  persecution under, 54
Neill, A. S., 115

Nemon, O., 7–9, 11, 54, 56–60, 63–69, 72–76, 83, 93, 99, 106, 109, 110
Nemon-Stuart, A., 68
Neumann, O., *see* Nemon, O.

Olga Studio, Vienna, 16, 17, 18, 27
Oppenheimer, R., 72, 110

Paris Psychoanalytical Society, 66
part-objects, 89
Peckham House mental hospital, London, 110
Peierls, R., 110
Phillips, J., 2
phthisis, 16
Picasso, P., 82
Pick, D., 2
Pietzner, C., 18, 19, 56
Pietzner Studio, Vienna, 18–24
Planck, M., 72
play technique, 1
portraiture, qualities of, 5–10
psychotic patients, treatment of, 1
psychotic states of mind, 1

Quinodoz, J.-M., 5, 41, 114

Radó, S., 49
Ravel, M., 10
Read, R., 11, 99
Reizes, Emanuel, 3, 13–16, 23, 24, 26–29, 32, 61, 62, 101
Reizes, Emily, 13–16
Reizes, M., 13–15, 27, 28
Reizes, S., 3, 13, 14, 61, 101
rheumatic heart disease, 16
Riviere, J., 60, 90, 91, 93, 94, 99, 100–102
Rosenberg (Ruzomberok), Slovakia, 26, 30, 31, 46
Russell, B., 117

Sachsel, B., 70–73, 83, 118, 120
Sargent, J. S., 9

Sayers, J., 3, 4, 14, 16, 24, 25, 28, 29, 32, 45, 78, 89, 90, 94–96, 98, 99, 101, 102
scarlet fever, 16
Schling, B., 40
Schmideberg, M., *née* Klein, 29–33, 46, 47, 62
Schmideberg, W., 46, 49, 62
Schonfeld, I., 29
Schubert, F., 72
scrofula, 14
Sebba, A., 60
Second World War, 43, 54, 81
    see also National Socialism/Nazism
Segal, H., 2–4, 10, 24, 41, 68, 69, 105, 108
Senator, R., 60
Severn, E., 76
Sharp, N., 93
Shavit, N., 111
Shenley psychiatric hospital, Hertfordshire, 111
Sherwin-White, S., 16, 23, 54
Singh, A., 90–93
Sitwell, E., 110
Slade School of Fine Art, London, 85, 86, 88, 93–95
Soames, M., 9, 10
Spira, M., 41, 114
Steiner, J., 99, 102
Stokes, Adrian, 11, 62, 78, 81, 88–90, 93–102, 109, 111, 113
Stokes, Ann, 96, 97, 99, 108
Stonebridge, L., 2, 91, 93, 100
Stoneman, W., 87
Stonor, J., 64, 65, 67
Strachey, A., 47
Strauss, R., 56
Stuart, F., 58
Summerhill School, Suffolk, 115
Sutherland, G., 9, 10, 96
Swiss Federal Technical High School, Zurich, 24

Sylvestor, D., 95
Sylwan, B., 29
Szabó, J., 37, 38, 39
Székely, A., 40–43, 51, 54, 72, 101
Székely, L., 42, 43
Székely-Kovács, O., *see* Dormandi, O.

Tate Collection, London, 90, 98
Tatra Mountains/Carpathian
     Mountains, 4, 61
Tavistock Clinic, Hampstead, 59
Temple of Universal Ethics, 59
Thorner, H., 104, 110–115
Topolski, D., 104
Topolski, F., 104–110, 112
Toruk, M., 29
Townsend, W., 87, 94–96
Treaty of Trianon, 1920, 46
tuberculosis, 14, 16, 54, 73

Uglow, E., 88
UN Relief and Rehabilitation
     Administration, Germany, 81
Ustaše, 60

Vienna, Klein in, 13–28
Vienna Art Academy, 56

Vienna Psychoanalytic Society, 48, 59
Villiers-Stuart, P., 63

Wakatsuki, J., 72
War Artists Advisory Committee, 82,
     86
Warbotz (Verbotz), Slovakia, 13
War Office, 92
Warsaw Art Academy, 104
Wellcome Library, 69
Westwood, E. R., 105
Wilde, O., 7
Williams, R. V., 82
Wimmer Studio, Vienna, 14, 15, 17
Winnicott, C., 63
Winnicott, D. W., 57
Wollfheim, N., 47, 78
Wollheim, R., 10
Wood, J., 59
Woolf, V., 61, 79

Yevonde, Madame [Yevonde
     Middleton], 117
Young, A., 9, 54, 56, 58–60, 63, 64, 67,
     68

Zec, D., 68